A-Z STEVENAGE

CONTENTS

Ind...
Vill...
sele...

REFERENCE

Motorway	**A1(M)**	Car Park Selected	P
A Road	A602	Church or Chapel	†
Proposed		Cycle Route	⊕⊘
B Road	B656	Fire Station	■
Dual Carriageway		Hospital	Ⓗ
One-way Street		House Numbers A & B Roads only	94 11
Traffic flow on A Roads is indicated by a heavy line on the driver's left.	→	Information Centre	🆔
Restricted Access		National Grid Reference	525
Pedestrianized Road		Police Station	▲
Residential Walkway	…………	Post Office	★
Track		Toilet	▽
Footpath		With facilities for the Disabled	♿
Local Authority Boundary		Educational Establishment	⌐
Postcode Boundary		Hospital or Hospice	⌐
Railway	Station 🚉	Industrial Building	⌐
Built-up Area	WEST LA.	Leisure or Recreational Facility	⌐
		Place of Interest	⌐
Map Continuation	▲ 10	Public Building	⌐
		Shopping Centre or Market	⌐
		Other Selected Buildings	⌐

Scale

1:15,840

4 inches (10.16 cm) to 1 mile
6.31cm to 1km

0   ¼   ½ Mile

0   250   500   750 Metres

Copyright of Geographers' A-Z Map Company Ltd.

Head Office:
Fairfield Road, Borough Green, Sevenoaks, Kent, TN15 8PP
Telephone 01732 781000 (General Enquiries & Trade Sales)

Showrooms:
44 Gray's Inn Road, London, WC1X 8HX
Telephone 020 7440 9500 (Retail Sales)
www.a-zmaps.co.uk

Ordnance Survey® This product includes mapping data licensed from Ordnance Survey® with the permission of the Controller of Her Majesty's Stationery Office.

C000194750

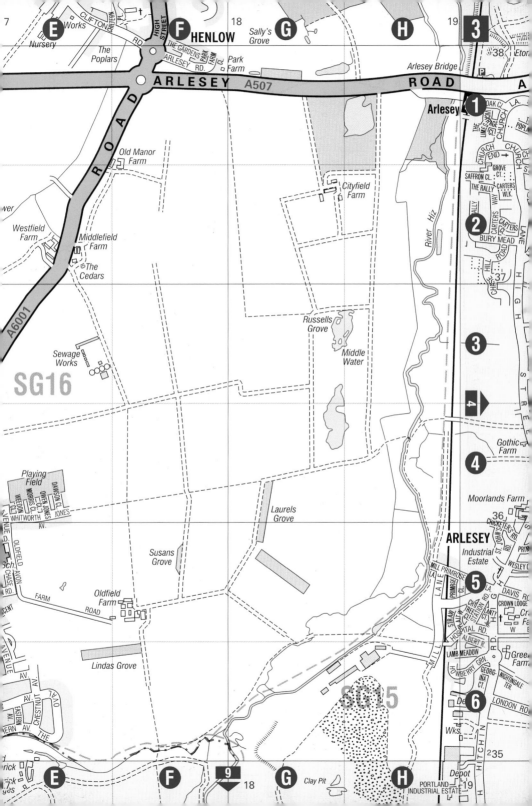

4

19

38

Arlesey Bridge

A

B

520

C

D

Etonbury

ARLESEY RD. /A507 ARLESEY - STOTFOLD

Waterloo Farm

1

Arlesey

OLD OAK CL.

THE LIMES

VICARAGE

CHURCH LA.

STOTFOLD

Pix

Nursery

Brook

THE POPLARS

CHASE CL.

LANE

STOTFOLD ROAD

Playing Field

THE LIMES

CHURCH END

CHURCH CHASE

SAFFRON CL.

GROVE CT.

ST. PETER'S AV.

Works

Swim. Pool

Tennis Courts

THE RALLY

CARTERS WLK.

GLEBE AV.

CHURCH END

Etonbury Middle School

2

CARTERS WAY

CARTERS

THE RALLY

BURY MEAD

HILL ROAD

HIGH HOUSE LANE

Chase Farm

River Hiz

37

CHASE

3

THE CHASE

3

STREET

LYMANS

COX'S WAY

GOTHIC WAY

EVEREST

ROAD

HILLARY RISE

SG15

Pix

Brook

4

HIGH

LYNTON AV.

Gothic Farm

Lib.

Schools

Comm. Cen.

Shawmer Farm

36

Moorlands Farm

CRICKETERS RD.

ST. JOHN'S RD.

PRIMROSE

HAWK WY.

WESLEY CL.

Playing Field

Industrial Estate

5

MILL

PRIMROSE CL.

PRIMROSE LA.

DAVIS ROW

ARLESEY

STATION RD.

CANTY

CHY.

A507 BY-PASS

HITCH...

ROAD

ARLESEY

Crown Lodge

Crown Farm

STRAW

HOSPITAL RD.

ALBERT R.

LAMB MEADOW

W E S T

Green Farm

Pig Developme Unit

MILL LANE

NEWBERRY GRN.

GEORG-INA CT.

NIGHTINGALE TER.

D R I V E

Tennis Court

Lodge

6

Depot

LONDON ROW

HITCHIN ROAD

Wks.

Sewage Works

Reservoir (Covered)

Cricket Ground

Bowling Green

235

A

Depot

19

B

520

10

C

D

PORTLAND INDUSTRIAL ESTATE

HITCHIN

Green Lagoon

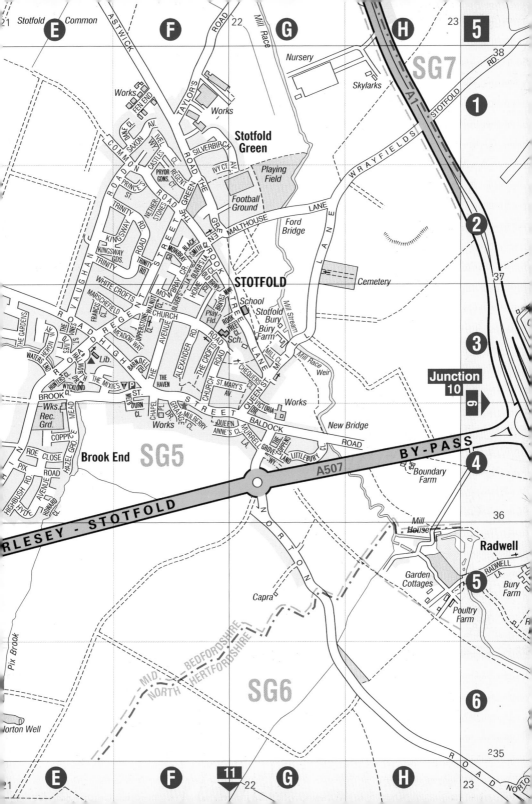

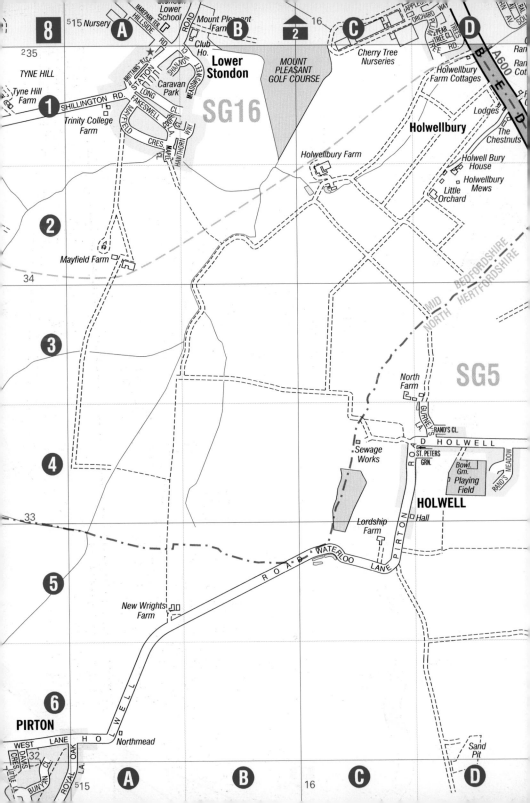

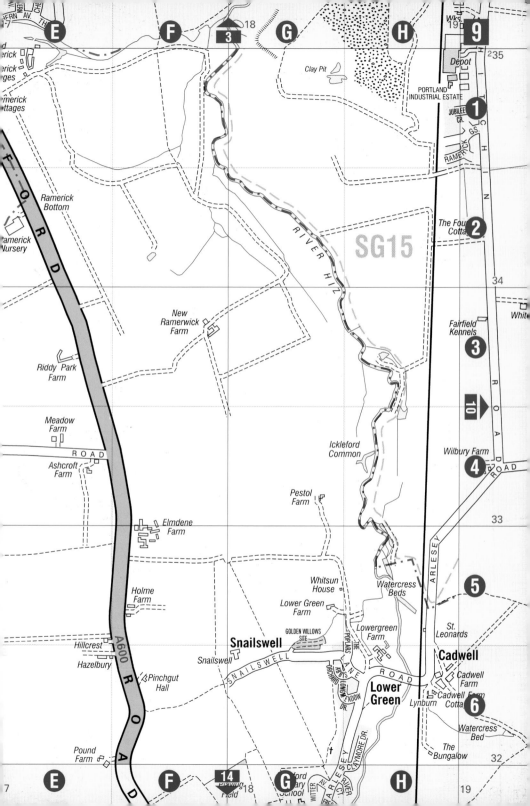

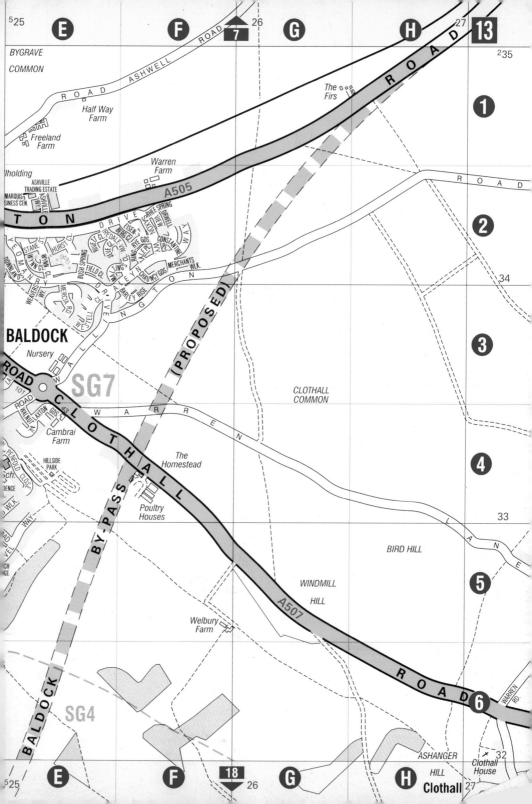

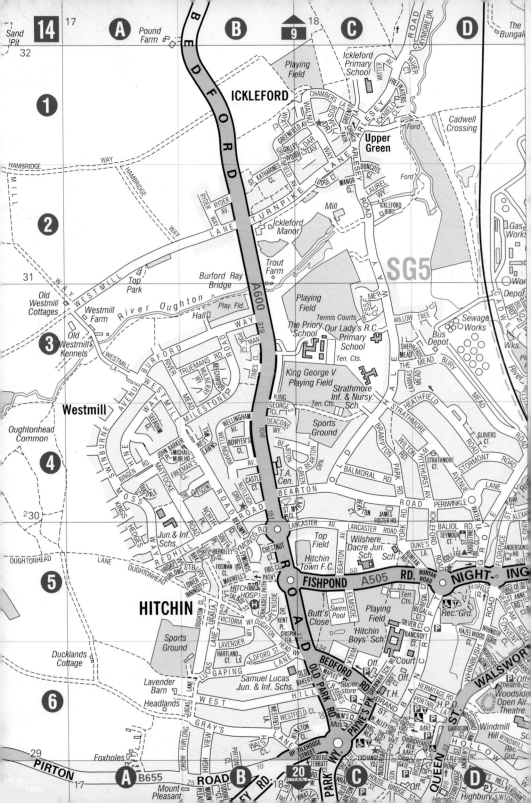

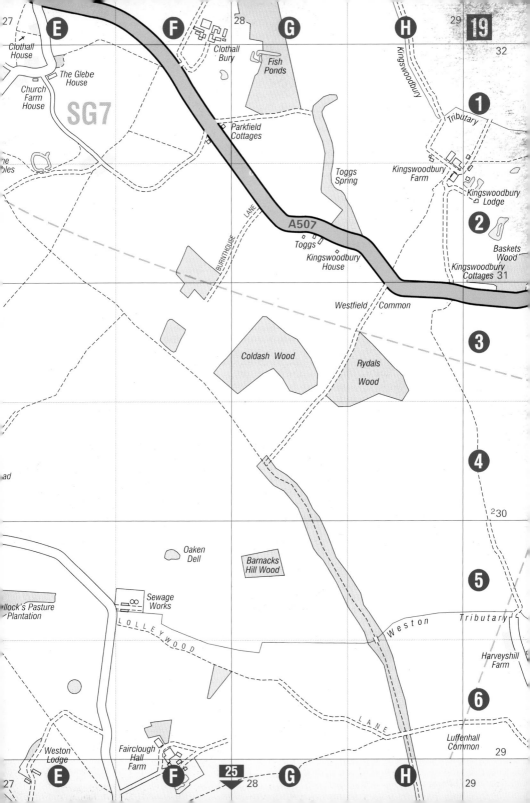

E
Clothall
House

F
Clothall
Bury

G
Fish
Ponds

H

27

28

29

32

Kingswoodbury

The Glebe
House

Church
Farm
House

SG7

Parkfield
Cottages

1

Tributary

Kingswoodbury
Farm

Kingswoodbury
Lodge

Toggs
Spring

LANE

A507

Toggs

Kingswoodbury
House

2

Baskets
Wood

Kingswoodbury
Cottages 31

BURNTHOUSE

Westfield Common

3

Coldash Wood

Rydals
Wood

4

²30

Oaken
Dell

Barnacks
Hill Wood

llock's Pasture
Plantation

Sewage
Works

5

Weston Tributary

LOLLEYWOOD

Harveyshill
Farm

ad

LANE

6

Luffenhall
Common

Weston
Lodge

Fairclough
Hall
Farm

E

F

25

G

H

29

27

28

29

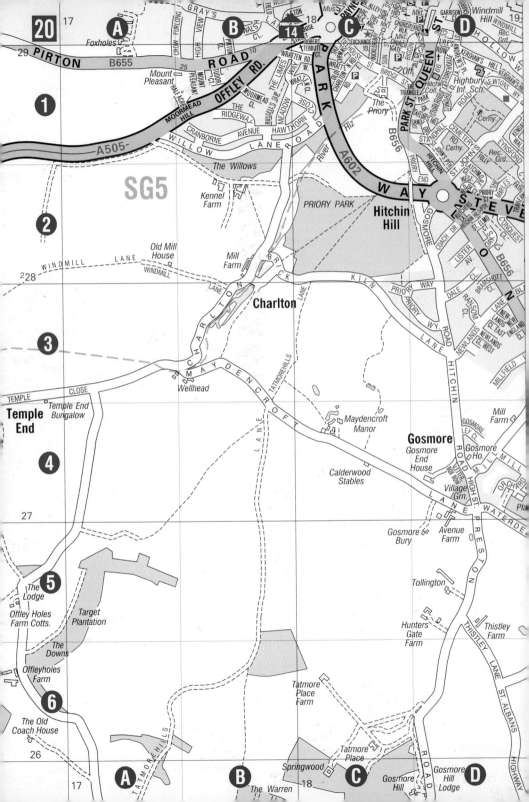

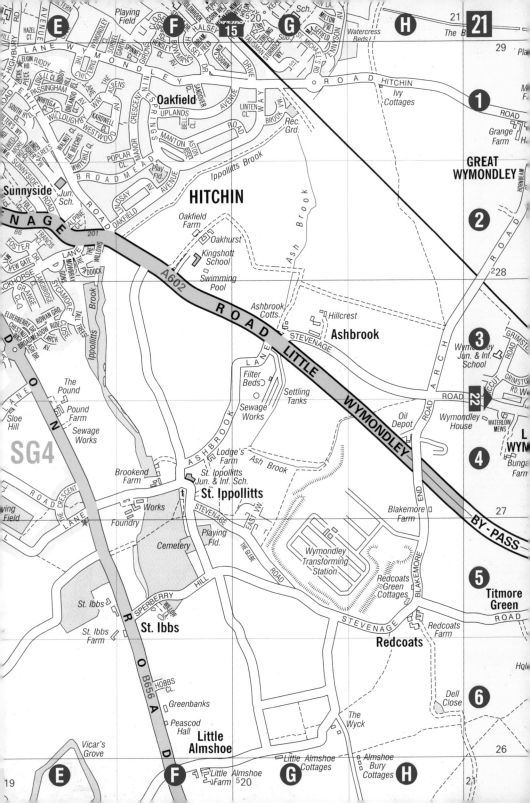

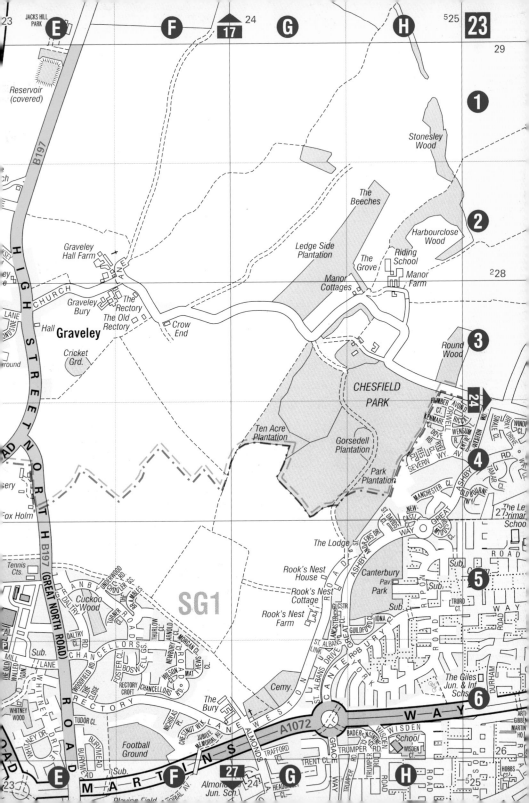

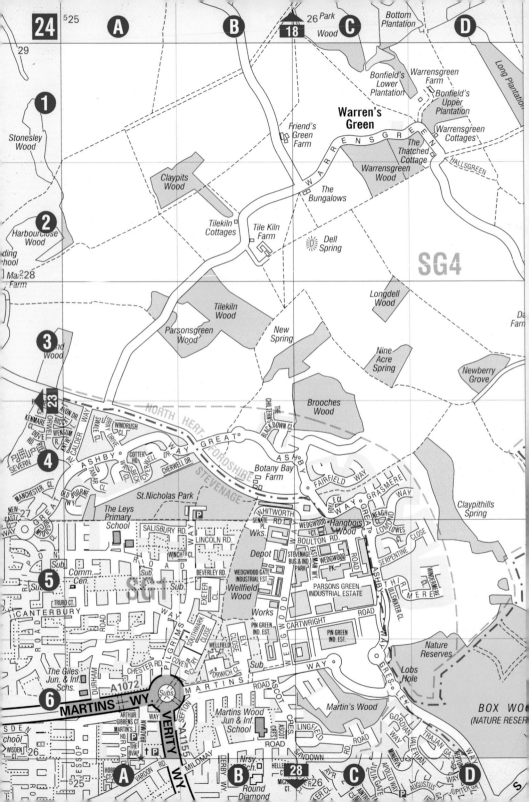

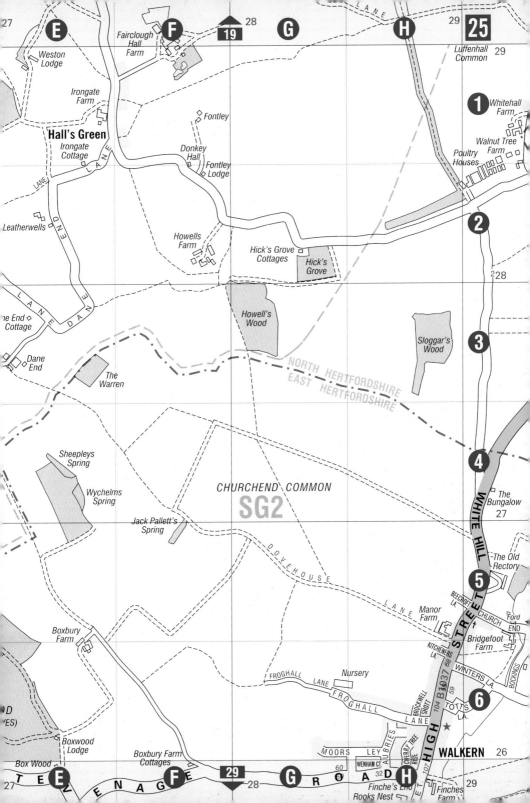

Fairclough Hall Farm

Luffenhall Common 29

Weston Lodge

1 Whitehall Farm

Irongate Farm

Fontley

Walnut Tree Farm

Hall's Green

Irongate Cottage

Donkey Hall

Poultry Houses

LANE

Fontley Lodge

LANE

2

Leatherwells

Howells Farm

Hick's Grove Cottages

Hick's Grove

228

DANE END

LANE

Howell's Wood

Sloggar's Wood

3

ne End Cottage

Dane End

NORTH HERTFORDSHIRE

EAST HERTFORDSHIRE

The Warren

4

Sheepleys Spring

WHITE HILL

The Bungalow 27

Wychelms Spring

CHURCHEND COMMON

SG2

The Old Rectory

Jack Pallett's Spring

5

DOVEHOUSE

BEECROFT LA

Manor Farm

STREET

CHURCH

Ford END

LANE

KITCHENERS LA

Bridgefoot Farm

WINTERS LA

Boxbury Farm

FROGHALL   LANE

Nursery

BROCKWELL SHOTT

B1037

104

59

BROCKINGS

6

FROGHALL   LANE

TOTTS LA

Boxwood Lodge

HIGH

Boxbury Farm Cottages

MOORS

WENHAM CT.

AUBRIES

CHERRY TREE RISE

32

STREET

WALKERN 26

Box Wood

60

107

Finche's End Rooks Nest

Finches Farm

▼

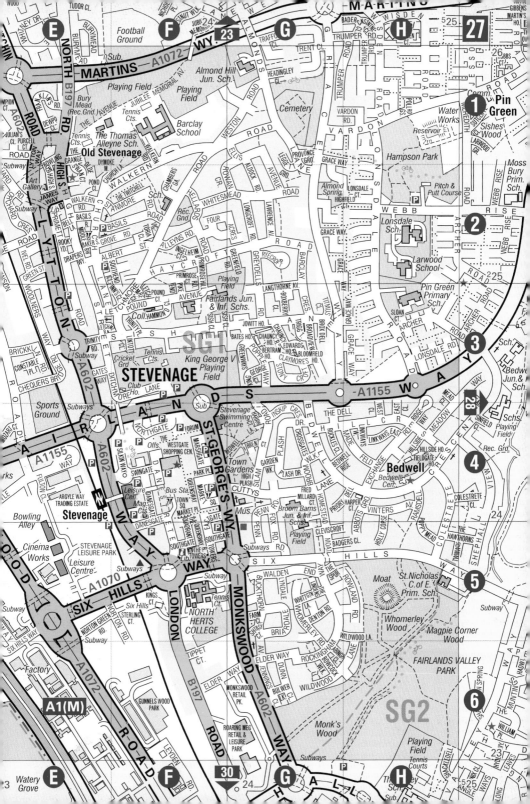

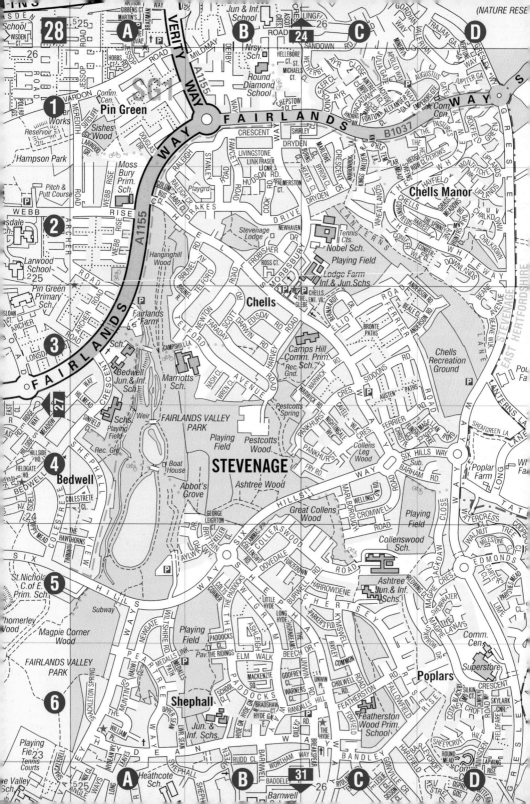

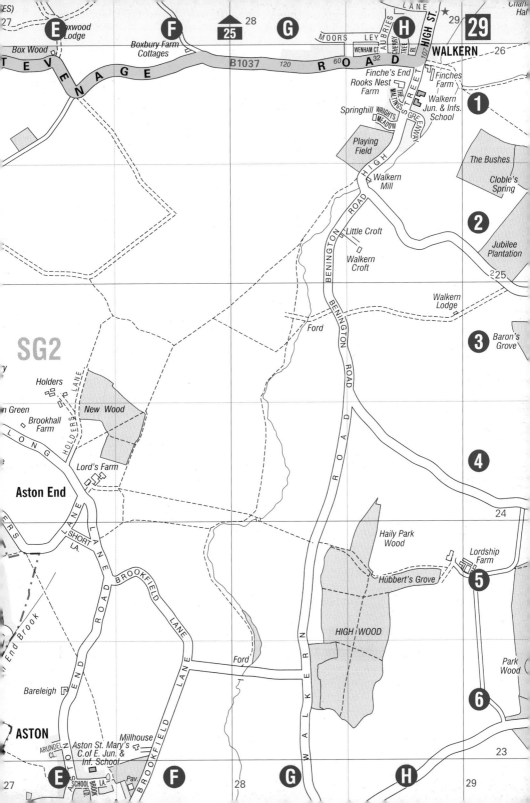

ES) 27

E Boxwood Lodge

Box Wood

S TEVENAGE

F

Boxbury Farm Cottages

28
25

G

MOORS LEY

WENHAM CT.

AUBRIES

CHERRY TREE RI

H HIGH ST. 29
★

WALKERN 26

ROAD

B1037 120 60 32

29

Chan Hal

Finche's End
Rooks Nest Farm

Springhill WRIGHTS MEADOW

Finches Farm

THE MALLINGS

STREET

HIGH

GWIN

GRE

Walkern Jun. & Infs. School

1

Playing Field

Walkern Mill

BENINGTON ROAD

The Bushes

Cloble's Spring

2

Jubilee Plantation

225

Little Croft
Walkern Croft

Ford

BENINGTON ROAD

Walkern Lodge

3 Baron's Grove

SG2

Holders

HOLDERS LANE

New Wood

Brookhall Farm

LONG

Lord's Farm

Aston End

4

24

Haily Park Wood

Lordship Farm

SHORT LA.

LANE

BROOKFIELD LANE

ROAD END

Hubbert's Grove

5

HIGH WOOD

Park Wood

End Brook

WALKERN

Bareleigh

6

ASTON

ARUNDEL CL.

Millhouse

Aston St. Mary's C.of E. Jun. & Inf. School

Ford

T

BROOKFIELD LANE

E SCHOOL LA.

Pav.

F

28

G

23

H

27

29

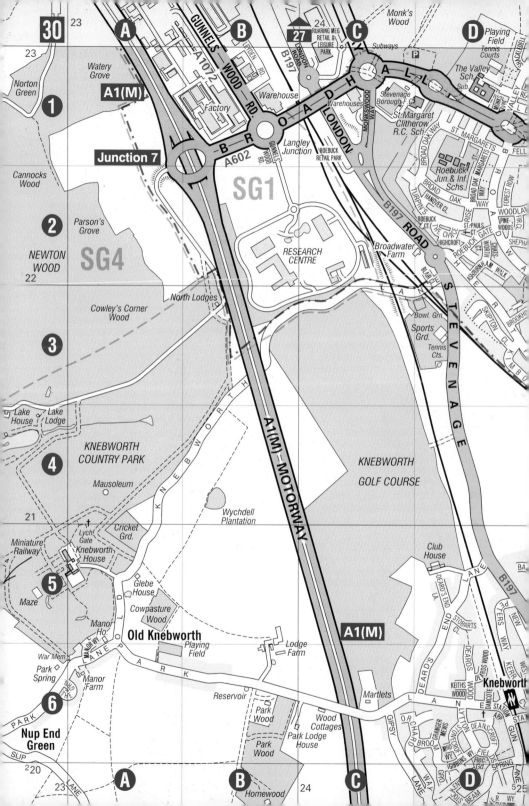

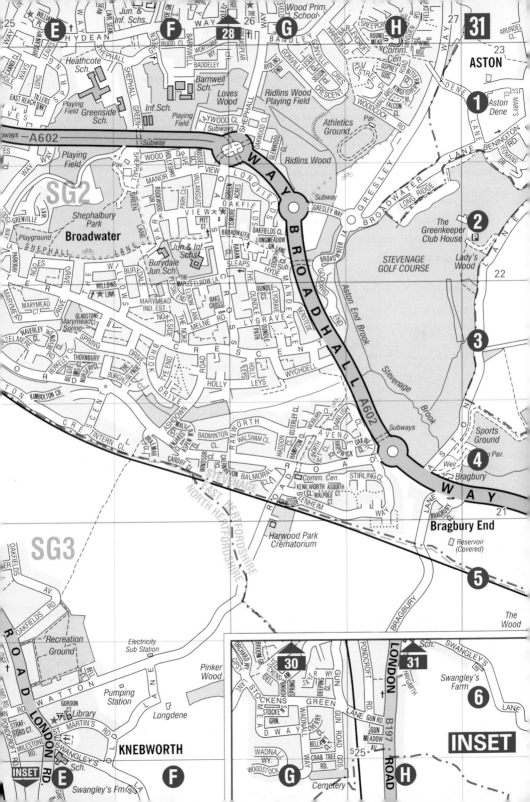

INDEX

Including Streets, Places & Areas, Hospitals & Hospices, Industrial Estates,
Selected Flats & Walkways and Selected Places of Interest.

HOW TO USE THIS INDEX

1. Each street name is followed by its Posttown or Postal Locality and then by its map reference; e.g. Abbotts Rd. *Let* —5D **10** is in the Letchworth Posttown and is to be found in square 5D on page **10**. The page number being shown in bold type.
A strict alphabetical order is followed in which Av., Rd., St., etc. (though abbreviated) are read in full and as part of the street name; e.g. Ash Dri. appears after Ashdown Rd. but before Ashleigh.

2. Streets and a selection of Subsidiary names not shown on the Maps, appear in the index in *Italics* with the thoroughfare to which it is connected shown in brackets; e.g. *Appletrees. Hit* —1C **20** (off Wratten Rd. W.)

3. Places and areas are shown in the index in **bold type**, the map reference to the actual map square in which the town or area is located and not to the place name; e.g. **Baldock. —3D 12**

4. An example of a selected place of interest is Athletics Ground. —1G 31

5. An example of a hospital or hospice is GARDEN HOUSE HOSPICE. —6H 11

GENERAL ABBREVIATIONS

All : Alley
App : Approach
Arc : Arcade
Av : Avenue
Bk : Back
Boulevd : Boulevard
Bri : Bridge
B'way : Broadway
Bldgs : Buildings
Bus : Business
Cvn : Caravan
Cen : Centre
Chu : Church
Chyd : Churchyard
Circ : Circle
Cir : Circus
Clo : Close
Comn : Common
Cotts : Cottages

Ct : Court
Cres : Crescent
Cft : Croft
Dri : Drive
E : East
Embkmt : Embankment
Est : Estate
Fld : Field
Gdns : Gardens
Gth : Garth
Ga : Gate
Gt : Great
Grn : Green
Gro : Grove
Ho : House
Ind : Industrial
Info : Information
Junct : Junction
La : Lane

Lit : Little
Lwr : Lower
Mc : Mac
Mnr : Manor
Mans : Mansions
Mkt : Market
Mdw : Meadow
M : Mews
Mt : Mount
Mus : Museum
N : North
Pal : Palace
Pde : Parade
Pk : Park
Pas : Passage
Pl : Place
Quad : Quadrant
Res : Residential
Ri : Rise

Rd : Road
Shop : Shopping
S : South
Sq : Square
Sta : Station
St : Street
Ter : Terrace
Trad : Trading
Up : Upper
Va : Vale
Vw : View
Vs : Villas
Vis : Visitors
Wlk : Walk
W : West
Yd : Yard

POSTTOWN AND POSTAL LOCALITY ABBREVIATIONS

Arl : Arlesey
Ast : Aston
Ast E : Aston End
Bald : Baldock
B'tn : Benington
Byg : Bygrave
Clot : Clothall
Clot C : Clothall Common
Cro : Cromer
D'wth : Datchworth

Gos : Gosmore
G'ley : Graveley
Gt Wym : Great Wymondley
Henl : Henlow
Hinx : Hinxworth
Hit : Hitchin
Hol : Holwell
Ickl : Ickleford
Kneb : Knebworth
Let : Letchworth

L Wym : Little Wymondley
L Ston : Lower Stondon
Newn : Newnham
Odsey : Odsey
Old K : Old Knebworth
Pir : Pirton
Pres : Preston
Radw : Radwell
St I : St Ippolyts
Shef : Shefford

Shil : Shillington
Stev : Stevenage
Stot : Stotfold
Up Ston : Upper Stondon
Walk : Walkern
W'ton : Weston
W'ian : Willian

INDEX

Abbis Orchard. *Ickl* —6G **9**
Abbots Gro. *Stev* —5H **27**
Abbotts Rd. *Let* —5D **10**
Abinger Clo. *Stev* —6G **27**
Acre Piece. *Hit* —1E **21**
Aintree Way. *Stev* —1C **28**
Alban Rd. *Let* —2E **17**
Albert Rd. *Arl* —5A **4**
Albert St. *Stev* —2E **27**
Aldeburgh Clo. *Stev* —6C **22**
Alder Clo. *Bald* —4C **12**
Aldock Rd. *Stev* —2G **27**
Aldridge Ct. *Bald* —2C **12**
Alexander Ga. *Stev* —1C **28**
Alexander La. *Stot* —3F **5**
Alexandra Rd. *Hit* —4D **14**

Aleyn Way. *Bald* —2F **13**
Alington La. *Let* —2B **16**
 (in two parts)
Alleyns Rd. *Stev* —2F **27**
Allison. *Let* —6A **12**
Almonds La. *Stev* —6G **23**
Alpine Clo. *Hit* —2E **21**
Alton Rd. *Henl* —5C **2**
Amor Way. *Let* —5H **11**
Anchor Rd. *Bald* —4D **12**
Anderson Rd. *Stev* —3D **28**
Andersons Ho. *Hit* —5D **14**
Angle Ways. *Stev* —1E **31**
Angotts Mead. *Stev* —3D **26**
Ansell Ct. *Stev* —6D **22**
Apollo Way. *Stev* —1C **28**

Applecroft. *L Ston* —6D **2**
Appletrees. Hit —1C **20**
 (off Wratten Rd. W.)
Arcade, The. *Hit* —6C **14**
Arcade, The. *Let* —5F **11**
Arcade Wlk. *Hit* —6C **14**
Archer Rd. *Stev* —3H **27**
Archers Way. *Let* —5D **10**
Arches, The. *Let* —4G **11**
Arch Rd. *Gt Wym* —3H **21**
Arden Press Way. *Let* —5H **11**
Arena Pde. *Let* —5F **11**
Argyle Way. *Stev* —4E **27**
Argyle Way Trad. Est. *Stev*
                          —4E **27**
Arlesey. —5A 4

Arlesey Rd. *Arl & Stot* —2D **4**
 (Hitchin Rd.)
Arlesey Rd. *Arl & Let* —5H **9**
 (Stotfold Rd.)
Arlesey Rd. *Henl* —1F **3**
 (in two parts)
Arlesey Rd. *Ickl* —2C **14**
Arlesey-Stotfold By-Pass. *Arl &*
                    Stot —1A **4**
Armour Ri. *Hit* —3F **15**
Arnold Clo. *Hit* —5F **15**
Arnold Clo. *Stev* —5F **23**
Arthur Gibbens Ct. *Stev* —6A **24**
Arundel Clo. *Ast* —6E **29**
Arwood M. *Bald* —3D **12**
Ascot Cres. *Stev* —6B **24**

Cavell Wlk. *Stev* —4C **28**
Cavendish Rd. *Stev* —4C **26**
Caxton Ga. *Stev* —5D **26**
Caxton Way. *Stev* —5D **26**
Cedar Av. *Ickl* —1C **14**
Cemetery Rd. *Hit* —1D **20**
Central Av. *Henl* —6D **2**
Chace, The. *Stev* —2D **30**
Chadwell Rd. *Stev* —5D **26**
Chagney Clo. *Let* —5E **11**
Chalkden Path. *Hit* —5B **14**
Chalkdown. *Stev* —2D **28**
Chalk Fld. *Let* —2E **17**
Chalk Hills. *Bald* —6D **12**
Chambers Ga. *Stev* —2F **27**
Chambers La. *Ickl* —1C **14**
Chancellors Rd. *Stev* —6E **23**
Chantry La. *Hit* —5B **22**
Chaomans. *Let* —2B **16**
Chapel Pl. *Stot* —4F **5**
Chapel Row. Hit —5D 14
  (off Whinbush Rd.)
Chapman Rd. *Stev* —6D **22**
Chapmans, The. *Hit* —1C **20**
Charlton. —3B 20
Charlton Rd. *Hit* —3B **20**
Chase Clo. *Arl* —1A **4**
Chase Hill Rd. *Arl* —3A **4**
Chase, The. *Arl* —3A **4**
Chasten Hill. *Let* —4D **10**
Chatsworth Ct. *Stev* —2D **30**
Chatterton. *Let* —6H **11**
Chaucer Way. *Hit* —5G **15**
Chauncy Gdns. *Bald* —2F **13**
Chauncy Ho. *Stev* —3G **27**
Chauncy Rd. *Stev* —3G **27**
Chells. —3B 28
Chells Enterprise Village. *Stev*
  —3C **28**
Chells La. *Stev* —2C **28**
  (in two parts)
Chells Manor. —2D 28
Chells Recreation Ground.
  —3D **28**
Chells Way. *Stev* —2A **28**
Chennells Clo. *Hit* —3F **15**
Chepstow Clo. *Stev* —1B **28**
Chequers Bri. Rd. *Stev* —3E **27**
Chequers Clo. *Stot* —3G **5**
Cherry Clo. *Kneb* —6G **31**
Cherry Tree Clo. *Arl* —5A **4**
Cherry Tree Ri. *Walk* —6H **25**
Cherry Trees. *L Ston* —6D **2**
Chertsey Ri. *Stev* —5C **28**
Cherwell Dri. *Stev* —4A **24**
Chesfield Downs Family Golf
  Cen. —5F 17
Chesfield Pk. —3H **23**
Chester Rd. *Stev* —6A **24**
Chestnut Av. *Henl* —6D **2**
Chestnut Ct. *Hit* —5B **14**
Chestnut Wlk. *St I* —3E **21**
Chestnut Wlk. *Stev* —6F **23**
Chiltern Pl. *Henl* —1F **3**
Chiltern Rd. *Bald* —5D **12**
Chiltern Rd. *Hit* —6E **15**
Chilterns, The. *Hit* —1E **21**
Chilterns, The. *Stev* —4B **24**
Chiltern Vw. *Let* —6D **10**
Chilvers Bank. *Bald* —4C **12**
Cholwell Rd. *Stev* —6C **28**
Chouler Gdns. *Stev* —5E **23**
Christie Rd. *Stev* —4C **28**
Church End. —2A 4
  (Arlesey)
Church End. —4D 18
  (Weston)
Church End. *Arl* —1A **4**

Church End. *Walk* —5H **25**
Churchgate. *Hit* —1C **20**
Church Grn. *Gt Wym* —1A **22**
Church La. *Arl* —1A **4**
Church La. *G'ley* —3E **23**
Church La. *Stev* —2E **27**
Church La. *W'ton* —5D **18**
Church La. *W'ian* —2A **12**
Church Path. *Ickl* —1C **14**
Church Path. *L Wym* —4B **22**
Church Rd. *Stot* —3F **5**
Church St. *Bald* —2C **12**
Church Yd. *Hit* —6C **14**
Churchyard Wlk. *Hit* —6C **14**
Clare Cres. *Bald* —5C **12**
Claymore Dri. *Ickl* —6H **9**
Claymores. *Stev* —3G **27**
Clevisscroft. *Stev* —5G **27**
Clifton Rd. *Henl* —1E **3**
Cloister Lawn. *Let* —1B **16**
Cloisters Rd. *Let* —1B **16**
Close, The. *Bald* —4C **12**
Close, The. *Stev* —6E **23**
Clothall. —1E 19
Clothall Rd. *Bald* —3D **12**
Clovelly Way. *Stev* —1C **26**
Coach Dri. *Hit* —2D **20**
Coach Ho. Cloisters. *Bald*
  —3C **12**
Coachman's La. *Bald* —3B **12**
Codicote Ho. Stev —6E 23
  (off Coreys Mill La.)
Coleridge Clo. *Hit* —5F **15**
Colestrete. *Stev* —5H **27**
Colestrete Clo. *Stev* —4A **28**
College Rd. *Hit* —5D **14**
Collenswood Rd. *Stev* —5B **28**
Collison Clo. *Hit* —3G **15**
Colonnade, The. Let —5F 11
  (off Eastcheap)
Colts Corner. *Stev* —5B **28**
Columbus Clo. *Stev* —2A **28**
Colwyn Clo. *Stev* —2D **26**
Commerce Way. *Let* —5F **11**
Common Ri. *Hit* —4E **15**
Common Rd. *Stot* —1F **5**
Common Vw. *Let* —3G **11**
Common Vw. Sq. *Let* —3G **11**
Conifer Clo. *Stev* —2D **28**
Conifer Wlk. *Stev* —2C **28**
Conquest Clo. *Hit* —2D **20**
Constantine Clo. *Stev* —6H **23**
Constantine Pl. *Bald* —2F **13**
Convent Clo. *Hit* —5D **14**
Cook Rd. *Stev* —2B **28**
Cooks Way. *Hit* —4E **15**
Cooper Clo. *L Ston* —1A **8**
Coopers Clo. *Stev* —5D **28**
Coopers Fld. *Let* —4D **10**
Coppens, The. *Stot* —4G **5**
Coppice Mead. *Stot* —4E **5**
Corey's Mill. —6D 22
Coreys Mill La. *Stev* —6D **22**
Corner Clo. *Let* —5E **11**
Cornfields. *Stev* —2C **28**
Corton Clo. *Stev* —1D **26**
Cotney Clo. *Stev* —6D **28**
Cotter Ho. *Stev* —4A **24**
Cotton Brown Pk. *Let* —4A **12**
Coventry Clo. *Stev* —6A **24**
Cowslip Hill. *Let* —4E **11**
Cox's Way. *Arl* —3A **4**
Crabbes Clo. *Hit* —6C **14**
Crabtree Dell. *Let* —2E **17**
Crabtree La. *Bald* —5C **12**
Crab Tree Rd. *Kneb* —6G **31**
Cragside. *Stev* —4G **31**
Cranborne Av. *Hit* —1B **20**

Cranborne Ct. Stev —6D 22
  (off Ingleside Dri.)
Creamery Ct. *Let* —2E **17**
Crescent, The. *Henl* —5D **2**
Crescent, The. *Hit* —4B **14**
Crescent, The. *Let* —6G **11**
Crescent, The. *St I* —4E **21**
Cricketer's Rd. *Arl* —5A **4**
Crispin Ter. *Hit* —5B **14**
Croft Ct. *Hit* —6C **14**
Croft La. *Let* —2G **11**
Crofts, The. *Stot* —3F **5**
Crompton Rd. *Stev* —3C **26**
Cromwell Grn. *Let* —3H **11**
Cromwell Rd. *Let* —3H **11**
Cromwell Rd. *Stev* —4C **28**
Crossgates. *Stev* —4G **27**
Crossleys. *Let* —1F **11**
Cross St. *Let* —4F **11**
Crow Furlong. *Hit* —1B **20**
Crown Lodge. *Arl* —5A **4**
Cubitt Clo. *Hit* —6G **15**
Curlew Clo. *Let* —2E **11**
Cuttys La. *Stev* —4G **27**

Dacre Rd. *Hit* —5E **15**
Dagnalls. *Let* —3B **16**
Daisy Ct. *Let* —3G **11**
Dale Clo. *Hit* —3D **20**
Dale, The. *Let* —6E **11**
Daltry Clo. *Stev* —5E **23**
Daltry Rd. *Stev* —5E **23**
Damask Clo. *W'ton* —5B **18**
Damask Green. —5B 18
Damask Grn. Rd. *W'ton* —5B **18**
Dancote. *Kneb* —6D **30**
Dane Clo. *Stot* —1F **5**
Dane End Ho. Stev —6E 23
  (off Coreys Mill La.)
Dane End La. *Hit* —3E **25**
Danescroft. *Let* —2F **11**
Danesgate. *Stev* —5F **27**
Daneshill Ho. Stev —4F 27
  (off Danestrete)
Danestrete. *Stev* —4F **27**
Darwin Rd. *Stev* —3B **28**
David Evans Ct. *Let* —4D **10**
Davis Cres. *Pir* —6A **8**
Davis Row. *Arl* —5A **4**
Dawlish Clo. *Stev* —4G **31**
Dawson Clo. *Henl* —4E **3**
Deacons Way. *Hit* —4B **14**
Deanscroft. *Kneb* —6D **30**
Deard's End La. *Kneb* —5D **30**
Deards Wood. *Kneb* —6D **30**
Deeping Clo. *Kneb* —6G **31**
Dell, The. *Bald* —5C **12**
Dell, The. *Stev* —4G **27**
Denby. *Let* —1D **16**
Dene La. *Ast* —1H **31**
Denton Rd. *Stev* —5G **27**
Dents Clo. *Let* —2E **17**
Derby Way. *Stev* —1B **28**
Derwent Rd. *Henl* —5D **2**
Desborough Rd. *Hit* —5G **15**
Devonshire Clo. *Stev* —3E **31**
Dewpond Clo. *Stev* —1E **27**
Diamond Ind. Cen. *Let* —4A **12**
Ditchmore La. *Stev* —3F **27**
Doncaster Clo. *Stev* —1C **28**
Douglas Dri. *Stev* —1A **28**
Dovedale. *Stev* —5B **28**
Dovehouse La. *Stev* —5G **25**
Dove Rd. *Stev* —4H **23**
Dower Ct. Hit —2D 20
  (off London Rd.)
Downlands. *Bald* —2E **13**

Downlands. *Stev* —2D **28**
Drakes Dri. *Stev* —2B **28**
Drapers Way. *Stev* —2E **27**
Dryden Cres. *Stev* —1B **28**
Dugdale Ct. *Hit* —4A **14**
Duke's La. *Hit* —5D **14**
Duncots Clo. *Ickl* —2C **14**
Dunham's La. *Let* —4H **11**
Dunlin. *Let* —2E **11**
Dunn Clo. *Stev* —6G **27**
Durham Rd. *Stev* —6A **24**
Dyes La. *Hit* —5A **26**
Dymoke M. *Stev* —1E **27**

Eagle Ct. *Bald* —2C **12**
Earlsmead. *Let* —2B **16**
Eastbourne Av. *Stev* —3C **26**
Eastcheap. *Let* —5F **11**
East Clo. *Hit* —4F **15**
East Clo. *Stev* —4H **27**
Eastern Av. *Henl* —6E **3**
Eastern Way. *Let* —3G **11**
Eastgate. *Stev* —5F **27**
Easthall Ho. Stev —5E 23
  (off Coreys Mill La.)
Eastholm. *Let* —3G **11**
Eastholm Grn. *Let* —3G **11**
Eastman Way. *Stev* —5C **24**
East Reach. *Stev* —1E **31**
East Vw. *St I* —5G **21**
Edgeworth Clo. *Stev* —2G **31**
Edison Rd. *Stev* —3B **28**
Edmonds Dri. *Stev* —5D **28**
Edwards Ho. *Stev* —3G **27**
Eisenberg Clo. *Bald* —2F **13**
Elbow La. *Stev* —3F **31**
Eldefield. *Let* —4C **10**
Elderberry Dri. *St I* —3E **21**
Elder Way. *Stev* —6F **27**
Elgin Ho. *Hit* —1E **21**
Eliot Rd. *Stev* —3C **28**
Ellice. *Let* —1D **16**
Ellis Av. *Stev* —1G **27**
Elm Pk. *Bald* —3D **12**
Elms Clo. *L Wym* —4A **22**
Elmside Wlk. *Hit* —5C **14**
Elm Wlk. *Stev* —6B **28**
Elmwood Av. *Bald* —4D **12**
Elmwood Ct. *Bald* —3D **12**
Ely Clo. *Stev* —5B **24**
Emperors Ga. *Stev* —1D **28**
Enjakes Clo. *Stev* —4F **31**
Ennsmore Clo. *Let* —2D **16**
Essex Ho. *Stev* —3D **26**
Essex Rd. *Stev* —1D **26**
Everest Clo. *Arl* —4B **4**
Exchange Rd. *Stev* —4H **27**
Exchange Yd. *Hit* —6C **14**
Exeter Clo. *Stev* —5B **24**
Eynsford Ct. *Hit* —1D **20**

Fairfield Way. *Hit* —5H **15**
Fairfield Way. *Stev* —4C **24**
Fairlands Valley Park. —6H 27
  (Shephall)
Fairlands Valley Pk. —4A 28
  (Stevenage)
Fairlands Way. *Stev* —4E **27**
Fairview Rd. *Stev* —1D **26**
Fakeswell La. *L Ston* —1A **8**
Falcon Clo. *Stev* —1H **31**
Fallowfield. *Stev* —6C **28**
Faraday Rd. *Stev* —3B **28**
Farm Clo. *Let* —2G **11**
Farm Clo. *Stev* —5G **27**
Farriers Clo. *Bald* —2C **12**

Hitchin Rd.—Manchester Clo.

Hitchin Rd. *Gos* —3D **20**
Hitchin Rd. *Henl* —5D **2**
Hitchin Rd. *Hit* —1H **21**
Hitchin Rd. *Let* —2A **16**
Hitchin Rd. *Shef* —1A **2**
Hitchin Rd. *Stev* —5D **22**
Hitchin Rd. *Stot* —6D **4**
Hitchin Rd. *W'ton* —3G **17**
Hitchin St. *Bald* —3C **12**
Hitchin Town F.C. —5C **14**
Hobbs Clo. *Hit* —6F **21**
Hobbs Ct. *Stev* —1A **28**
Holdbrook. *Hit* —6F **15**
Holden Clo. *Hit* —6G **15**
Holders La. *Ast E* —4E **29**
Hollow La. *Hit* —6D **14**
Holly Copse. *Stev* —5H **27**
Holly Leys. *Stev* —3F **31**
Hollyshaws. *Stev* —1F **31**
Holmdale. *Let* —6G **11**
Holroyd Cres. *Bald* —4C **12**
Holwell. —4D 8
Holwell. Stev —5E 23
 (off Coreys Mill La.)
Holwellbury. —1D 8
Holwell Rd. *Hol* —4D **8**
Holwell Rd. *Pir* —6A **8**
Home Clo. *Stev* —3F **5**
Homestead Moat. *Stev* —4G **27**
Hoo Rd. *Shef* —2A **2**
Hopewell Rd. *Bald* —3B **12**
Hopton Rd. *Stev* —2C **26**
Horace Gay Gdns. *Let* —6E **11**
Hornbeam Ct. *Gt Wym* —2A **22**
Hornbeam Spring. *Kneb* —6G **31**
Hornbeams, The. *Stev* —5B **28**
Hospital Rd. *Arl* —5H **3**
House La. *Arl* —2A **4**
Howard Clo. *Stot* —4E **5**
Howard Ct. *Let* —1D **16**
Howard Gardens. —6G **11**
Howard Ga. *Let* —1D **16**
Howard Pk. —5G **11**
Howard Pk. Corner. *Let* —5G **11**
Howards Wood. *Let* —2D **16**
Howberry Grn. *Arl* —6H **3**
Hudson Rd. *Stev* —2B **28**
Humber Ct. *Stev* —4H **23**
Hunters Clo. *Stev* —2D **28**
Hunters Clo. *Stot* —3E **5**
Huntingdon Rd. *Stev* —1D **26**
Hunting Ga. *Hit* —2E **15**
Hurst Clo. *Bald* —2E **13**
Hyatt Trad. Est. *Stev* —4C **26**
Hydean Way. *Stev* —6A **28**
Hyde Av. *Stot* —4E **5**
Hyde Grn. E. *Stev* —6B **28**
Hyde Grn. N. *Stev* —6B **28**
Hyde Grn. S. *Stev* —6B **28**
Hyde, The. *Stev* —6C **28**

Ibberson Way. *Hit* —6E **15**
Ickleford. —1C 14
Ickleford. Stev —5E 23
 (off Coreys Mill La.)
Ickleford Bury. *Ickl* —2C **14**
Ickleford Rd. *Hit* —4D **14**
Icknield Clo. *Ickl* —1C **14**
Icknield Grn. *Let* —5C **11**
Icknield Way. *Bald* —2C **12**
Icknield Way. *Let* —5C **10**
Icknield Way E. *Bald* —2D **12**
Ingelheim Ct. *Stev* —2F **27**
Ingleside Dri. *Stev* —5C **22**
Inn's Clo. *Stev* —3F **27**
Inskip Cres. *Stev* —4G **27**
Iona Clo. *Stev* —5H **23**

Iredale Vw. *Bald* —2E **13**
Ivatt Ct. *Hit* —6G **15**
Ivel Ct. *Let* —1E **17**
Ivel Rd. *Stev* —2E **27**
Ivel Way. *Bald* —5E **13**
Ivel Way. *Stot* —1F **5**
Ivy Ct. *Stot* —2F **5**

Jackdaw Clo. *Stev* —5D **28**
Jackman's Pl. *Let* —5H **11**
Jacks Hill Pk. *G'ley* —6E **17**
Jackson St. *Bald* —2C **12**
James Foster Ho. *Hit* —4C **14**
James Way. *Stev* —2E **27**
Jarden. *Let* —1E **17**
Jay Clo. *Let* —3E **11**
Jennings Clo. *Stev* —6G **27**
Jessop Rd. *Stev* —1A **28**
Jeve Clo. *Bald* —2E **13**
Jill Grey Pl. *Hit* —1D **20**
John Barker Pl. *Hit* —4A **14**
John Henry Leisure Cen.
 —6D **22**
Jowitt Ho. *Stev* —3G **27**
Jubilee Cres. *Arl* —1H **9**
Jubilee Memorial Av. *Stev*
 (in two parts) —1F **27**
Jubilee Rd. *Let* —4A **12**
Jubilee Rd. *Stev* —1D **26**
Jubilee Trade Cen. *Let* —4B **12**
Julia Ga. *Stev* —1C **28**
Julian's Clo. *Stev* —1E **27**
Julian's Rd. *Stev* —1D **26**
Jupiter Ga. *Stev* —1D **28**

Kardwell Clo. *Hit* —1E **21**
Keats Clo. *Stev* —2C **28**
Keats Way. *Hit* —6G **15**
Keiths Wood. *Kneb* —6D **30**
Keller Clo. *Stev* —5B **28**
Kendale Rd. *Hit* —1D **20**
Kenilworth Clo. *Stev* —4G **31**
Kenmare Clo. *Stev* —4H **23**
Kennet Way. *Stev* —4A **24**
Kent Pl. *Hit* —5B **14**
Kerr Clo. *Kneb* —6D **30**
Kershaw's Hill. *Hit* —1D **20**
 (in two parts)
Kessingland Av. *Stev* —6C **22**
Kestrel Clo. *Stev* —1H **31**
Kestrel Wlk. *Let* —2D **16**
Kimberley. *Let* —2F **11**
Kimbolton Cres. *Stev* —3D **30**
Kimpton. Stev —5E 23
 (off Coreys Mill La.)
Kingfisher Clo. *Hit* —1E **21**
Kingfisher Ct. *Let* —3E **11**
Kingfisher Ri. *Stev* —1H **31**
King George Clo. *Stev* —3G **27**
King George V Playing Field.
 —3B **14**
King Georges Clo. *Hit* —3B **14**
Kings Ct. *Stev* —5F **27**
Kingsdown. *Hit* —1F **21**
Kings Hedges. *Hit* —4A **14**
 (in two parts)
King's Rd. *Hit* —5D **14**
Kings Walden Ri. *Stev* —2C **28**
Kingsway. *Stot* —2F **5**
Kingsway Gdns. *Stot* —2E **5**
Kingswood Av. *Hit* —4H **15**
Kipling Clo. *Hit* —6G **15**
Kitcheners La. *Walk* —6H **25**
Kitching La. *Stev* —4B **26**
Kite Way. *Let* —3E **11**
Kiwi Ct. *Hit* —4D **14**

Knap Clo. *Let* —3A **12**
Knebworth. —6E 31
Knebworth Golf Course. —4C **30**
Knebworth House. —5A **30**
Knights Templar La. *Stev* —1C **28**
Knowle. *Stev* —6D **22**
Knowl Piece. *Hit* —2E **15**
Kristiansand Way. *Let* —3A **12**
Kymswell Rd. *Stev* —5C **28**
Kyrkeby. *Let* —1E **17**

Lacre Way. *Let* —4A **12**
Lamb Mdw. *Arl* —6H **3**
Lammas Mead. *Hit* —3C **14**
Lammas Path. *Stev* —5B **28**
Lammas Way. *Let* —3F **11**
Lancaster Av. *Hit* —5C **14**
Lancaster Clo. *Stev* —5G **23**
Lancaster Rd. *Hit* —5C **14**
Langbridge Clo. *Hit* —2E **21**
Langleigh. *Let* —2F **11**
Langthorne Av. *Stev* —3G **27**
Lannock. *Let* —1F **17**
Lannock Hill. *Let* —3F **17**
Lanterns. *Stev* —2C **28**
Lanterns La. *Ast E* —3D **28**
Lanthony Ct. *Arl* —5A **4**
Lapwing Dell. *Let* —3D **16**
Lapwing Ri. *Stev* —6D **28**
Larch Av. *St I* —3E **21**
Larkins Clo. *Bald* —2D **12**
Larkinson. *Stev* —2E **27**
Larwood Gro. *Stev* —1A **28**
Latchmore Clo. *Hit* —2D **20**
Laurel M. *Bald* —2D **12**
Laurel Way. *Ickl* —2C **14**
Lavender Ct. *Bald* —2C **12**
Lavender Way. *Hit* —6B **14**
Lawns, The. *Stev* —5D **28**
Lawrence Av. *Let* —1C **16**
Lawrence Av. *Stev* —2G **27**
Lawrence Mead. *L Wym* —3B **22**
Laxton Gdns. *Bald* —4E **13**
Leas, The. *Bald* —4C **12**
Leaves Spring. *Stev* —1D **30**
Leggett Gro. *Stev* —1G **27**
Leslie Clo. *Stev* —1G **31**
Letchmore Clo. *Stev* —3F **27**
Letchmore Rd. *Stev* —3F **27**
 (in two parts)
Letchworth. —5F 11
Letchworth Bus. & Retail Pk.
 Let —4A **12**
Letchworth Ga. *Let* —6H **11**
Letchworth Golf Course. —3A **16**
Letchworth La. *Let* —2B **16**
Letchworth Mus. & Art Gallery.
 —6F **11**
Letchworth Rd. *Bald* —3B **12**
Letchworth Shop. Cen. *Let*
 —5F **11**
Letchworth Swimming Pool.
 —4G **11**
Letter Box Row. *Gos* —4D **20**
Leyden Rd. *Stev* —6F **27**
Leys Av. *Let* —5F **11**
Lime Clo. *Stev* —5D **28**
Limekiln La. *Bald* —4D **12**
Limes, The. *Arl* —1A **4**
Limes, The. *Hit* —1B **20**
Lincoln Rd. *Stev* —5B **24**
Lindencroft. *Let* —2G **11**
Lindens, The. *Stev* —5G **27**
Lindsay Av. *Hit* —2F **21**
Lingfield Rd. *Stev* —6C **24**
Link, The. *Let* —2G **11**
Linkways E. *Stev* —4H **27**

Linkways W. *Stev* —4H **27**
Linnet Clo. *Let* —3E **11**
Lintern Clo. *Hit* —1G **21**
Lintott Clo. *Stev* —3F **27**
Lismore. *Stev* —2G **31**
Lister Av. *Hit* —2D **20**
Lister Clo. *Stev* —5E **23**
 (off Coreys Mill La.)
LISTER HOSPITAL. —5D **22**
Little Almshoe. —6F 21
Littlebury Clo. *Stot* —4G **5**
Little Hyde. *Stev* —5B **28**
Little La. *Pir* —6A **8**
 (in two parts)
Little Wymondley. —4B 22
Lit. Wymondley By-Pass. *Hit* &
 Stev —3G **21**
Livingstone Link. *Stev* —1B **28**
Lodge Ct. *Ickl* —2C **14**
Lodge Way. *Stev* —2E **31**
Lolleywood La. *Hit* —5F **15**
Lomond Way. *Stev* —5C **24**
London Rd. *Bald* —5D **12**
 (in two parts)
London Rd. *Gos*
 —2D **20** & 5A **26**
London Rd. *Kneb* —6E **31**
London Rd. *Stev* —5F **27**
London Row. *Arl* —6A **4**
Long Clo. *L Ston* —1A **8**
Longcroft Rd. *Stev* —2G **27**
Longfield. *Stev* —1D **26**
Longfield Ct. *Let* —4D **10**
Longfields. *Stev* —2G **31**
Long Hyde. *Stev* —5B **28**
Long La. *Ast E* —4D **28**
Long Leaves. *Stev* —1E **31**
Longmead. *Let* —4E **11**
Longmeadow Dri. *Ickl* —6G **9**
Longmeadow Grn. *Stev* —2G **31**
Long Ridge. *Ast* —2H **31**
Lonsdale Ct. *Stev* —2H **27**
Lonsdale Rd. *Stev* —1H **27**
Lordship La. *Let* —1D **16**
Lovell Clo. *Hit* —1E **21**
Lower Green. —6H 9
Lower Innings. *Hit* —5B **14**
Lower Sean. *Stev* —6A **28**
Lower Stondon. —6C 2
Lower Titmore Green. —6A 22
Lowes Clo. *Stev* —5C **24**
Lucas La. *Hit* —5B **14**
Lygrave. *Stev* —3G **31**
Lyle's Row. *Hit* —1D **20**
Lymans Rd. *Arl* —3A **4**
Lymington Rd. *Stev* —1D **26**
Lyndale. *Stev* —5G **27**
Lynton Av. *Arl* —4A **4**
Lytton Av. *Let* —6F **11**
Lytton Fields. *Kneb* —6D **30**
Lytton Way. *Stev* —2E **27**

Macfadyen Webb Ho. *Let*
 —4G **11**
Mackenzie Sq. *Stev* —6B **28**
Maddles. *Let* —1F **17**
Made Feld. *Stev* —4H **27**
Magellan Clo. *Stev* —4D **28**
Magpie Cres. *Stev* —5D **28**
Maiden St. *W'ton* —4B **18**
Mallard Rd. *Stev* —1H **31**
Malthouse La. *Stot* —2G **5**
Maltings Clo. *Bald* —2E **13**
Maltings, The. *Let* —2A **12**
Maltings, The. *Stev* —1H **29**
Malvern Clo. *Stev* —4F **31**
Manchester Clo. *Stev* —4H **23**

Mandeville. *Stev* —3G **31**
Manor Clo. *Ickl* —2C **14**
Manor Clo. *Let* —2B **16**
Manor Cres. *Hit* —1F **21**
Manor Ho. Dri. *Stev* —2D **28**
Manor Vw. *Stev* —2F **31**
Manor Way. *Let* —2B **16**
Manor Way. *Old K* —6A **30**
Mansfield Rd. *Bald* —4C **12**
Manton Rd. *Hit* —1F **21**
Maple Clo. *L Ston* —1A **8**
Maples Ct. *Hit* —6C **14**
Maples, The. *Hit* —2D **20**
Maples, The. *Stev* —2F **31**
Marcus Clo. *Stev* —1C **28**
Market Pl. *Hit* —6C **14**
Market Pl. *Stev* —4F **27**
Market Sq. *Stev* —4F **27**
Marlborough Clo. *W'ton* —5B **18**
Marlborough Rd. *Stev* —4C **28**
Marlowe Clo. *Stev* —1C **28**
Marmet Av. *Let* —5E **11**
Marquis Bus. Cen. *Bald* —2E **13**
Marschefield. *Stot* —3E **5**
Marshgate. *Stev* —4F **27**
Martin's Ho. *Stev* —6A **24**
Martins Way. *Stev* —1E **27**
Martin Way. *Let* —6D **10**
Marymead Ct. *Stev* —3E **31**
Marymead Dri. *Stev* —3E **31**
Marymead Ind. Est. *Stev* —3F **31**
Masefield. *Hit* —6G **15**
Matthew Ga. *Let* —2E **21**
Matthews Clo. *Stev* —6F **23**
Mattocke Rd. *Hit* —4A **14**
Maxwell Rd. *Stev* —4D **26**
Maxwell's Path. *Hit* —5B **14**
Maycroft. *Let* —2G **11**
Maydencroft La. *Gos* —3B **20**
Mayfield Cres. *L Ston* —1A **8**
Mayles Clo. *Stev* —2D **26**
Maylin Clo. *Hit* —5G **15**
Maytrees. *Hit* —1E **21**
Mead Clo. *Stev* —3H **27**
Meadow Bank. *Hit* —5F **15**
Meadowsweet. *L Ston* —1B **8**
Meadow Way. *Hit* —1B **20**
Meadow Way. *Let* —6F **11**
Meadow Way. *Stev* —4H **27**
Meadow Way. *Stot* —3F **5**
Meads, The. *Let* —5E **11**
Mead, The. *Hit* —3C **14**
Meadway. *Kneb* —6G **31**
Meadway. *Stev* —3D **26**
(Gunnels Wood Rd.)
Meadway. *Stev* —3C **26**
(Redcar Dri., in two parts)
Meadway Ct. *Stev* —3D **26**
Meadway Technology Pk. *Stev*
—3C **26**
Medalls Link. *Stev* —6A **28**
Medalls Path. *Stev* —6A **28**
Meeting Ho. La. *Bald* —2C **12**
Melbourn Clo. *Stot* —3F **5**
Melne Rd. *Stev* —3F **31**
Mercia Rd. *Bald* —3E **13**
Meredith Rd. *Stev* —1A **28**
Mermaid Clo. *Hit* —6F **15**
Mews, The. *Let* —2A **12**
Michael Muir Ho. *Hit* —4B **14**
Middlefields. *Let* —2F **11**
Middlefields Ct. Let —2F **11**
(off Middlefields)
Middle Row. *Stev* —2E **27**
Middlesborough Clo. *Stev*
—5H **23**
Middlesex Ho. *Stev* —3D **26**

Midhurst. *Let* —3F **11**
Mildmay Rd. *Stev* —1B **28**
Milestone Clo. *Stev* —5D **28**
Milestone Rd. *Hit* —4B **14**
Milestone Rd. *Kneb* —6E **31**
Milksey La. *Hit* —2E **23**
Millard Way. *Hit* —3G **15**
Mill Clo. *Hit* —5G **15**
Mill Clo. *Stot* —3G **5**
Millfield La. *St I* —3D **20**
Mill La. *Arl* —5H **3**
Mill La. *Gos* —4D **20**
Mill La. *Stot* —3G **5**
Mill La. *W'ton* —4C **18**
Mill Rd. *St I* —4D **20**
Millstream Clo. *Hit* —3D **14**
Mill Way. *Hit* —2A **14**
Milton Clo. *Let* —2D **16**
Milton Vw. *Hit* —6G **15**
Mindenhall Ct. Stev —2E **27**
(off High St.)
Minehead Way. *Stev* —2C **26**
Minerva Clo. *Stev* —6C **24**
Minsden Rd. *Stev* —6D **28**
Mixies, The. *Stot* —3E **5**
Mobbsbury Way. *Stev* —2B **28**
Monklands. *Let* —5D **10**
Monks Clo. *Stev* —5C **10**
Monks Vw. *Stev* —1D **30**
Monkswood Retail Pk. *Stev*
—6G **27**
Monkswood Way. *Stev* —5G **27**
Montfitchet Wlk. *Stev* —1D **28**
Moormead Clo. *Hit* —1B **20**
Moormead Hill. *Hit* —1A **20**
Moors Ley. *Walk* —6G **25**
Morecombe Clo. *Stev* —2D **26**
Morgan Clo. *Stev* —6F **23**
Morris Clo. *Henl* —4E **3**
Moss Way. *Hit* —4A **14**
Mount Garrison. *Hit* —6D **14**
Mountjoy. *Hit* —4G **15**
Mount Pleasant. *Hit* —1B **20**
Mount Pleasant Golf Course.
—6B **2**
Mowbray Cres. *Stot* —2F **5**
Mowbray Gdns. *Hit* —2E **21**
Mozart Ct. *Stev* —4E **27**
Muddy La. *Let* —2B **16**
Muirhead Way. *Kneb* —6D **30**
Mulberry Clo. *Stot* —4F **5**
Mulberry Way. *Hit* —3B **14**
Mullway. *Let* —5C **10**
Mundesley Clo. *Stev* —6D **22**
Muntings, The. *Stev* —6A **28**
Munts Mdw. *W'ton* —4C **18**
Murrell La. *Stot* —4G **5**

Narrowbox La. *Stev* —2C **28**
Nash Clo. *Stev* —3B **28**
Neagh Clo. *Stev* —4C **24**
Nene Rd. *Henl* —5D **2**
Neptune Ga. *Stev* —6D **24**
Netherstones. *Stot* —2F **5**
Netley Dell. *Let* —2D **16**
Nevell's Grn. *Let* —4F **11**
Nevells Rd. *Let* —5F **11**
Nevilles Ct. *Let* —3A **12**
Newbury Clo. *Stev* —6F **23**
Newcastle Clo. *Stev* —4H **23**
New Clo. *Kneb* —5D **30**
Newells. *Let* —1E **17**
Newells Way. *Let* —6B **12**
New England Clo. *St I* —3D **20**
Newgate. *Stev* —5A **28**
Newhaven. *Stev* —2B **28**
Newlands. *Let* —2C **16**

Newlands Clo. E. *Hit* —3D **20**
Newlands Clo. W. *Hit* —3D **20**
Newlands La. *Hit* —3D **20**
Newlyn Clo. *Stev* —3C **26**
Newnham. —2D 6
Newnham Hall. —1D **6**
Newnham Rd. *Bald* —2D **6**
New Rd. *Shef* —1C **2**
Newton Rd. *Stev* —3B **28**
Newtons Way. *Hit* —1D **20**
Nicholas Pl. *Stev* —6F **23**
Nightingale Ct. *Hit* —5E **15**
Nightingale Rd. *Hit* —5D **14**
Nightingale Ter. *Arl* —6A **4**
Nightingale Wlk. *Stev* —4C **28**
Nightingale Way. *Bald* —5C **12**
Nimbus Way. *Hit* —6G **15**
Ninesprings Way. *Hit* —1F **21**
Nodes Dri. *Stev* —2E **31**
Nokeside. *Stev* —3F **31**
Noke, The. *Stev* —3F **31**
Normans Clo. *Let* —2F **11**
North Av. *Let* —3H **11**
Northern Av. *Henl* —6D **2**
Northfields. *Let* —2F **11**
Northgate. *Stev* —4F **27**
North Herts Leisure Cen.
—5A **12**
North Pl. *Hit* —4B **14**
North Rd. *G'ley & Stev* —4E **23**
Norton. —2A 12
Norton Bury La. *Let* —1A **12**
Norton Common. —3F **11**
Norton Cres. *Bald* —3C **12**
Norton Green. —6D 26
Norton Grn. Rd. *Stev* —5E **27**
Norton Mill La. *Let & Hinx* —6B **6**
Norton Rd. *Let & Bald* —3G **11**
Norton Rd. *Stev* —5F **27**
Norton Rd. *Stot & Let* —5G **5**
Norton Way N. *Let* —5G **11**
Norton Way S. *Let* —5G **11**
Norwich Clo. *Stev* —6B **24**
Nun's Clo. *Hit* —6C **14**
Nup End Green. —6A 30
Nursery Clo. *Stev* —3E **31**
Nutleigh Gro. *Hit* —4B **14**

Oakfield. —2F **21**
Oakfield Av. *Hit* —2F **21**
Oakfields. *Stev* —2F **31**
Oakfields Av. *Kneb* —5E **31**
Oakfields Clo. *Stev* —2G **31**
Oakfields Rd. *Kneb* —5E **31**
Oakhill. *Let* —1F **17**
Oak La. *G'ley* —3D **22**
Oaks Clo. *Hit* —2D **20**
Oaks Cross. *Stev* —2F **31**
Oaktree Clo. *Let* —1A **16**
Oakwell Clo. *Stev* —4H **31**
Oakwood Clo. *Stev* —1G **31**
Offley Rd. *Hit* —1B **20**
Old Bakery. *Hit* —6C **14**
Old Bourne Way. *Stev* —4A **24**
Old Brewery Clo. *Stot* —2F **5**
Old Chantry. *Stev* —5C **22**
Old Charlton Rd. *Hit* —1C **20**
Olden Mead. *Let* —2D **16**
Olde Swan Ct. *Stev* —2E **27**
Oldfield Farm Rd. *Henl* —5D **2**
(in two parts)
Old Hale Way. *Hit* —4C **14**
Old Knebworth. —5A 30
Old Knebworth La. *Old K* —5A **30**
Old La. *Kneb* —6E **31**
Old Oak Clo. *Arl* —1A **4**
Old Pk. Rd. *Hit* —6C **14**

Old School Wlk. *Arl* —5A **4**
Old Stevenage. —2E 27
Old Walled Garden, The. *Stev*
—6E **23**
Oliver's La. *Stot* —3F **5**
(in two parts)
Olympus Rd. *Henl* —5D **2**
Openshaw Way. *Let* —5F **11**
Orchard Clo. *Let* —3F **11**
Orchard Clo. *St I* —4D **20**
Orchard Cres. *Stev* —2E **27**
Orchard Rd. *Bald* —2C **12**
Orchard Rd. *Hit* —4F **15**
Orchard Rd. *Stev* —2E **27**
Orchard, The. *Bald* —3D **12**
Orchard Vw. *Hit* —4F **15**
Orchard Way. *Kneb* —6C **30**
Orchard Way. *Let* —3F **11**
Orchard Way. *L Ston* —6D **2**
Ordelmere. *Let* —2F **11**
Orlando Clo. *Hit* —1E **21**
Orwell Av. *Stev* —4H **23**
Orwell Vw. *Bald* —2F **13**
Osbourne Ct. *Bald* —4D **12**
Osprey Gdns. *Stev* —1H **31**
Osterley Clo. *Stev* —4G **31**
Oughton Clo. *Hit* —5B **14**
Oughtonhead La. *Hit* —5A **14**
(in two parts)
Oughton Head Way. *Hit* —5B **14**
Oundle Ct. *Stev* —3G **31**
Oundle Path. *Stev* —3G **31**
Oundle, The. *Stev* —2G **31**
Oval, The. *Henl* —6E **3**
Oval, The. *Stev* —6A **24**
Owen Jones Clo. *Henl* —4E **3**
Oxleys Rd. *Stev* —6B **28**

Pacatian Way. *Stev* —1C **28**
Paddock Clo. *Let* —6G **11**
Paddocks Clo. *Stev* —5B **28**
Paddocks, The. *Stev* —5B **28**
Paddock, The. *Hit* —2E **21**
Page Clo. *Bald* —5D **12**
Palmerston Ct. *Stev* —2B **28**
Pankhurst Cres. *Stev* —4C **28**
Parade, The. Let —2F **11**
(off Southfields)
Parishes Mead. *Stev* —5D **28**
Park Clo. *Bald* —4C **12**
Park Clo. *Stev* —2F **31**
Park Ct. *Let* —5G **11**
Park Cres. *Bald* —4C **12**
Park Dri. *Bald* —4C **12**
Parker Clo. *Let* —1A **16**
Parker's Fld. *Stev* —5C **28**
Pk. Farm Clo. *Henl* —1F **3**
Parkfield. *Let* —1F **17**
Park Gdns. *Bald* —4C **12**
Park Ga. *Hit* —1D **20**
Park La. *Old K* —6A **30**
Park Pl. *Stev* —4F **27**
Park St. *Bald* —3C **12**
Park St. *Hit* —1C **20**
Park Vw. *Stev* —2F **31**
Park Way. *Hit* —1C **20**
Parkway. *Stev* —2E **31**
Parsons Grn. Ind. Est. *Stev*
—5C **24**
Pascal Way. *Let* —3H **11**
Passingham Av. *Hit* —1E **21**
Pasture Rd. *Let* —2A **16**
Pastures, The. *Stev* —1D **28**
Pastures, The. *Up Ston* —6A **2**
Paynes Clo. *Let* —2G **11**
Payne's Pk. *Hit* —6C **14**
Pearl Ct. *Bald* —3D **12**

Pearsall Clo. *Let* —6H **11**
Pear Tree Clo. *L Ston* —6D **2**
Pear Tree Dell. *Let* —2D **16**
Peartree Way. *Stev* —6A **28**
Pebbles, The. *Radw* —5A **6**
Peckworth Ind. Est. *L Ston*
—5C **2**
Pelican Way. *Let* —2F **11**
Pembroke Rd. *Bald* —3D **12**
Penfold Clo. *Bald* —4E **13**
Penn Rd. *Stev* —4G **27**
Penn Way. *Let* —2D **16**
Pepper All. *Bald* —3D **12**
Peppercorn Wlk. *Hit* —6F **15**
Pepper Ct. *Bald* —3C **12**
Pepsal End. *Stev* —3F **31**
Pepys Way. *Bald* —3C **12**
Periwinkle La. *Hit* —4D **14**
Peters Way. *Kneb* —5D **30**
Petworth Clo. *Stev* —4G **31**
Pike End. *Stev* —3F **27**
Pilgrims Way. *Radw* —6A **24**
PINEHILL HOSPITAL. —6F **15**
Pinewoods. *Stev* —2D **30**
Pin Green. —6A 24
Pin Green Ind. Est. *Stev* —5C **24**
(Cartwright Rd.)
Pin Grn. Ind. Est. *Stev* —5B **24**
(Wedgwood Way)
Pinnocks Clo. *Bald* —4D **12**
Pinnocks La. *Bald* —4D **12**
Pirton. —6A 8
Pirton Clo. *Hit* —6B **14**
Pirton Rd. *Hit* —1A **20**
Pirton Rd. *Hol* —5C **8**
Pitch And Putt Course. —2C **16**
(Letchworth)
Pitch And Putt Course. —2H **27**
(Stevenage)
Pitt Ct. *Stev* —2F **31**
Pixmore Av. *Let* —5H **11**
Pixmore Cen. *Let* —5G **11**
Pixmore Ind. Est. *Let* —5G **11**
Pixmore Way. *Let* —6F **11**
Pix Rd. *Let* —5G **11**
Pix Rd. *Stot* —4E **5**
Plash Dri. *Stev* —4G **27**
Plum Tree Rd. *L Ston* —6D **2**
Pollard Gdns. *Stev* —1H **27**
Pond Clo. *Stev* —2E **27**
Pondcroft Rd. *Kneb* —6E **31**
Pond La. *Bald* —3C **12**
Pondside. *G'ley* —3E **23**
Poplar Clo. *Hit* —1E **21**
Poplars. —6D 28
Poplars, The. *Arl* —1A **4**
Poplars, The. *Ickl* —5H **9**
Popple Way. *Stev* —3G **27**
Poppy Mead. *Stev* —5H **27**
Portland Ind. Est. *Arl* —1H **9**
Portman Clo. *Hit* —3B **14**
Portmill La. *Hit* —6D **14**
Post Office Row. *W'ton* —4B **18**
Potters La. *Stev* —5D **26**
Pound Av. *Stev* —3F **27**
Pound Ct. *Stev* —3F **27**
Prestatyn Clo. *Stev* —2D **26**
Preston Rd. *Gos* —5D **20**
Primary Way. *Arl* —5A **4**
Primett Rd. *Stev* —2E **27**
Primrose Clo. *Arl* —5H **3**
Primrose Ct. *Stev* —2F **27**
Primrose Hill Rd. *Stev* —2F **27**
Primrose La. *Arl* —5A **4**
Prince's St. *Stot* —2F **5**
Priory Ct. *Hit* —2D **20**
Priory Dell. *Stev* —4G **27**
Priory End. *Hit* —1D **20**

Priory La. *L Wym* —3B **22**
Priory Pk. —2C 20
Priory Vw. *L Wym* —3A **22**
Priory Way. *Hit* —3C **20**
Protea Ind. Est. *Let* —5H **11**
Protea Way. *Let* —5H **11**
Providence Gro. *Stev* —1G **27**
Providence Pl. *Bald* —4D **12**
Providence Way. *Bald* —4D **12**
Pryor Rd. *Bald* —4D **12**
Pryors Ct. *Bald* —2D **12**
Pryor Way. *Let* —1F **17**
Pullman Dri. *Hit* —6F **15**
Pulter's Way. *Hit* —1E **21**
Purcell Ct. *Stev* —1E **27**
Purwell. —5G 15
Purwell La. *Hit* —5G **15**
Pyms Clo. *Let* —3H **11**

Quadrant, The. *Let* —5F **11**
Quadrant, The. *Stev* —5F **27**
Queen Anne's Clo. *Stot* —4F **5**
Queen St. *Hit* —1D **20**
Queen St. *Stot* —3G **5**
Queensway. *Stev* —4F **27**
Queenswood Dri. *Hit* —4G **15**
Quills. *Let* —1F **17**
Quinn Way. *Let* —6A **12**

Raban Clo. *Stev* —2G **31**
Raban Ct. *Bald* —2D **12**
Radburn Corner. *Let* —6A **12**
Radburn Way. *Let* —1D **16**
Radcliffe Rd. *Hit* —5E **15**
Radwell. —5A 6
Radwell La. *Radw* —5A **6**
Raleigh Cres. *Stev* —1A **28**
Rally, The. *Arl* —2A **4**
(in two parts)
Ramerick Gdns. *Arl* —1H **9**
Ramsdell. *Stev* —4H **27**
Randalls Hill. *Stev* —6B **28**
Rand's Clo. *Hol* —4D **8**
Rand's Mdw. *Hol* —4D **8**
Ransom Clo. *Hit* —3D **20**
Ranworth Av. *Stev* —4G **31**
Rectory Cft. *Stev* —6F **23**
Rectory La. *Stev* —6E **23**
Redcar Dri. *Stev* —3C **26**
Redcoats. —5H 21
Redhill Rd. *Hit* —5A **14**
Redhoods Way E. *Let* —4E **11**
Redhoods Way W. *Let* —5E **11**
Redoubt Clo. *Hit* —4E **15**
Redwing Clo. *Stev* —5C **28**
Regal Ct. *Hit* —5G **14**
Regent Ct. *Stot* —2F **5**
Regent St. *Stot* —3F **5**
Reynolds. *Let* —2F **11**
Rhee Spring. *Bald* —2F **13**
Riccat La. *Stev* —4H **23**
Rickyard, The. *Let* —2A **12**
Riddell Gdns. *Bald* —3D **12**
Riddy Hill Clo. *Hit* —1E **21**
Riddy La. *Hit* —1E **21**
Ridge Av. *Let* —5G **11**
Ridge Rd. *Let* —5G **11**
Ridge, The. *Let* —5G **11**
Ridgeway. *Stev* —4H **27**
Ridgeway, The. *Hit* —1B **20**
Ridings, The. *Stev* —6B **28**
Ridlins End. *Stev* —1G **31**
Ringtale Pl. *Bald* —2F **13**
Ripon Rd. *Stev* —5H **23**
Rise, The. *Bald* —4C **12**
River Clo. *Ickl* —1D **14**

River Mead. *Hit* —3A **14**
Rivett Clo. *Bald* —2E **13**
Roaring Meg Retail &
Leisure Pk. *Stev* —6G **27**
Robert Humbert Ho. *Let* —6G **11**
Robert Saunders Ct. *Let* —1A **16**
Robert Tebbutt Ct. *Hit* —6C **14**
Robin Wlk. *Let* —2E **11**
Rockingham Way. *Stev* —6G **27**
Roebuck Ct. *Stev* —2D **30**
Roebuck Ga. *Stev* —2D **30**
Roebuck Retail Pk. *Stev* —1C **30**
Roe Clo. *Stot* —4E **5**
Roman La. *Bald* —3D **12**
Romany Clo. *Let* —5C **10**
Rookes Clo. *Let* —2D **16**
Rook Tree Clo. *Stot* —3F **5**
Rook Tree La. *Stot* —2F **5**
Rookwood Dri. *Stev* —2F **31**
Rooky Yd. *Stev* —2E **27**
Rosemont Clo. *Let* —5E **11**
Ross Ct. *Stev* —2B **28**
Round Mead. *Stev* —6D **28**
Roundwood Clo. *Hit* —3G **15**
Rowan Clo. *W'ton* —5B **18**
Rowan Cres. *Let* —4E **11**
Rowan Cres. *Stev* —2F **27**
Rowan Gro. *St I* —3E **21**
Rowans, The. *Bald* —4C **12**
Rowland Rd. *Stev* —5H **27**
Rowland Way. *Let* —5F **11**
Royal Oak La. *Pir* —6A **8**
Royston Rd. *Bald* —2D **12**
Ruckles Clo. *Stev* —4G **27**
Rudd Clo. *Stev* —6B **28**
Rudham Gro. *Let* —2E **17**
Rundells. *Let* —1F **17**
Runnalow. *Let* —4D **10**
Runswick Ct. *Stev* —2C **26**
Rushby Mead. *Let* —5G **11**
Rushby Pl. *Let* —6G **11**
Rushby Wlk. *Let* —5G **11**
Rush Green. —5A 26
Ruskin La. *Hit* —6G **15**
Russell Clo. *Stev* —1F **31**
Russell's Slip. *Hit* —1B **20**
Rutherford Clo. *Stev* —3C **26**
Ryder Av. *Ickl* —2B **14**
Ryder Way. *Ickl* —2B **14**
Rye Clo. *Stev* —4H **23**
Ryecroft. *Stev* —2G **27**
Rye Gdns. *Bald* —2F **13**
Ryley Clo. *Henl* —5D **2**

Saddlers Clo. *Bald* —3C **12**
(off Hitchin St.)
Saffron Clo. *Arl* —2A **4**
Saffron Hill. *Let* —5E **11**
St Albans Dri. *Stev* —6G **23**
St Albans Highway. *Pres* —6D **20**
St Albans Link. *Stev* —6G **23**
St Andrews Dri. *Stev* —5H **23**
St Andrew's Pl. *Hit* —6D **14**
St Annes Ct. *Hit* —5D **14**
St Anne's Rd. *Hit* —5D **14**
St Davids Clo. *Stev* —4H **23**
St Elmo Ct. *Hit* —2D **20**
St Faiths Clo. *Hit* —4F **15**
St George's Way. *Stev* —4F **27**
St Ibbs. —5E 21
St Ippollitts. —4F 21
St John's Path. *Hit* —1D **20**
St John's Rd. *Arl* —5A **4**
St John's Rd. *Hit* —2D **20**
St Katharines Clo. *Ickl* —2B **14**
St Margarets. *Stev* —1D **30**
St Mark's Clo. *Hit* —4B **14**

St Martin's Rd. *Kneb* —6E **31**
St Mary's Av. *Stot* —3F **5**
St Mary's Clo. *Ast* —1H **31**
St Mary's Clo. *Let* —3B **16**
St Mary's Way. *Bald* —5C **12**
St Michaels Ct. *Stev* —1B **28**
St Michael's Mt. *Hit* —5E **15**
St Michaels Rd. *Hit* —5F **15**
St Nicholas Pk. —4A **24**
St Olives. *Stot* —3E **5**
St Pauls Ct. *Stev* —2D **30**
St Peter's Av. *Arl* —2A **4**
St Peters Grn. *Hol* —4D **8**
Sale Dri. *Clot C* —2D **12**
Salisbury Rd. *Bald* —2C **12**
Salisbury Rd. *Stev* —5A **24**
Sanderling Clo. *Let* —3E **11**
Sandover Clo. *Hit* —1F **21**
Sandown Rd. *Stev* —6C **24**
Sandy Gro. *Hit* —1D **20**
Sanfoine Clo. *Hit* —5G **15**
Saunders Clo. *Let* —4A **12**
Sax Ho. *Let* —2E **11**
Saxon Av. *Stot* —1F **5**
Saxon Clo. *Let* —2F **11**
Saxon Way. *Bald* —2F **13**
Sayer Way. *Kneb* —6G **31**
Scarborough Av. *Stev* —1C **26**
School Clo. *Stev* —6B **28**
Schoolfields. *Let* —6A **12**
School La. *Ast* —6E **29**
School La. *W'ton* —4C **18**
School Wlk. *Let* —5H **11**
Scott Rd. *Stev* —3B **28**
Second Av. *Let* —5A **12**
Seebohm Clo. *Hit* —4A **14**
Sefton Rd. *Stev* —6B **24**
Senate Pl. *Stev* —4B **24**
Serpentine Clo. *Stev* —5C **24**
Severn Way. *Stev* —4H **23**
Seymour Ct. *Hit* —5D **14**
Shackledell. *Stev* —1D **30**
Shackleton Spring. *Stev* —6A **28**
Shaftesbury Ct. *Stev* —5G **27**
Shaftesbury Ind. Cen. *Let*
—4G **11**
Shannon Clo. *L Ston* —1A **8**
Sharps Way. *Hit* —4E **15**
Sheafgreen La. *Stev* —4D **28**
Shearwater Clo. *Stev* —5D **28**
Sheepcroft Hill. *Stev* —6D **28**
Shelley Clo. *Hit* —6G **15**
Shephalbury Pk. —2E **31**
Shephall. —6A 28
Shephall Grn. *Stev* —1E **31**
Shephall Grn La. *Stev* —1F **31**
Shephall La. *Stev* —2D **30**
(in two parts)
Shephall Vw. *Stev* —4A **28**
Shephall Way. *Stev* —5B **28**
Shepherds La. *Stev* —3B **26**
Shepherds Mead. *Hit* —3C **14**
Sheringham Av. *Stev* —6D **22**
Sherwood. *Let* —3F **11**
Shillington Rd. *Shil & L Ston*
—1A **8**
Shirley Clo. *Stev* —1B **28**
Shoreham Clo. *Stev* —1C **26**
Short La. *Stev* —5E **29**
Shott La. *Let* —5G **11**
Siccut Rd. *L Wym* —3A **22**
Siddons Rd. *Stev* —3C **28**
Silam Rd. *Stev* —4G **27**
Silkin Ct. *Stev* —6D **28**
Silkin Way. *Stev* —4F **27**
Silverbirch Av. *Stot* —1F **5**
Silver Ct. *Hit* —5C **14**
Simpson Dri. *Bald* —3D **12**

Simpsons Ct. *Bald* —3D **12**
Sinfield Clo. *Stev* —4A **28**
Sish Clo. *Stev* —3F **27**
(in two parts)
Sish La. *Stev* —3F **27**
Sisson Clo. *Stev* —1G **31**
Six Hills Way. *Stev* —6E **27**
Sixth Av. *Let* —5A **12**
Skegness Rd. *Stev* —1C **26**
Skipton Clo. *Stev* —3D **30**
Skylark Corner. *Stev* —6D **28**
Sleaps Hyde. *Stev* —2G **31**
Slip La. *Old K* —6A **30**
Sloan Ct. *Stev* —3H **27**
Snailswell. —6G 9
Snailswell La. *Ickl* —6G **9**
Snipe, The. *W'ton* —4B **18**
Sollershott E. *Let* —1B **16**
Sollershott Hall. *Let* —1B **16**
Sollershott W. *Let* —1A **16**
Sorrel Gdn. *Hit* —1E **21**
Souberie Av. *Let* —6F **11**
South Clo. *Bald* —4D **12**
Southend Clo. *Stev* —2F **27**
Southern Av. *Henl* —6D **2**
Southern Way. *Let* —2E **11**
Southfields. *Let* —2F **11**
Southgate. *Stev* —5F **27**
South Hill Clo. *Hit* —1E **21**
South Pl. *Hit* —5B **14**
South Rd. *Bald* —4D **12**
Southsea Rd. *Stev* —1D **26**
South Vw. *Let* —6F **11**
Southwark Clo. *Stev* —6B **24**
Southwold Clo. *Stev* —3C **26**
Sparhawke. *Let* —2G **11**
Sparrow Dri. *Stev* —5D **28**
Speke Clo. *Stev* —4D **28**
Spellbrooke. *Hit* —1F **21**
Sperberry Hill. *St I* —5F **21**
Spinney Clo. *Hit* —1F **21**
Spinney, The. *Bald* —4C **12**
Spinney, The. *Stev* —2D **28**
Sports Cen. —5F 15
(Hitchin)
Spreckley Clo. *Henl* —4D **2**
Spring Dri. *Stev* —3E **31**
Spring Rd. *Let* —5E **11**
Springshott. *Let* —6E **11**
Spurrs Clo. *Hit* —6F **15**
Spur, The. *Stev* —5G **27**
Standalone Farm Cen. —3D **10**
Standhill Clo. *Hit* —1D **20**
Standhill Rd. *Hit* —1D **20**
Stane Fld. *Let* —2D **16**
Stane St. *Bald* —2E **13**
Stanley Rd. *Stev* —1B **28**
Stanmore Rd. *Stev* —2F **27**
Station App. *Hit* —5E **15**
Station App. *Kneb* —6D **30**
Station Pde. Let —5F **11**
(off Station Rd.)
Station Pl. *Let* —5F **11**
Station Rd. *Arl* —5A **4**
Station Rd. *Kneb* —6D **30**
Station Rd. *Let* —5F **11**
Station Rd. *L Ston* —1A **8**
Station Rd. *Odsey* —2D **12**
Station Ter. *Hit* —5E **15**
Station Way. *Let* —5E **11**
Sterling Ct. *Stev* —5F **27**
Stevenage. —4F 27
Stevenage Borough F.C.
—1C **30**
Stevenage Bus. & Ind. Pk.
Stev —5C **24**
Stevenage Enterprise Cen.
Stev —2D **26**

Stevenage Golf Course. —2H **31**
Stevenage Leisure Cen. —4F **27**
Stevenage Leisure Pk. *Stev*
—5E **27**
Stevenage Mus. —4G **27**
Stevenage Rd. *Hit* —2D **20**
Stevenage Rd. *L Wym & Stev*
—3G **21**
Stevenage Rd. *St I* —4F **21**
Stevenage Rd. *Stev & Kneb*
—3D **30**
Stevenage Rd. *Walk* —1E **29**
Stevenage Swimming Cen.
—4F **27**
Stirling Clo. *Hit* —6G **15**
Stirling Clo. *Stev* —4H **31**
Stobarts Clo. *Kneb* —5D **30**
Stockens Dell. *Kneb* —6G **31**
Stockens Grn. *Kneb* —6G **31**
Stonecroft. *Kneb* —6D **30**
Stoneley. *Let* —2F **11**
Stonnells Clo. *Let* —3F **11**
Stony Cft. *Stev* —3G **27**
Storehouse La. *Hit* —1D **20**
Stormont Rd. *Hit* —4D **14**
Stotfold. —3F 5
Stotfold Green. —1F 5
Stotfold Rd. *Arl* —1A **4**
Stotfold Rd. *Bald* —1H **5**
Stotfold Rd. *Let* —4C **10**
Strafford Ct. *Kneb* —6E **31**
Strathmore Av. *Hit* —4C **14**
Strathmore Ct. *Hit* —4C **14**
Straw Plait W. *Arl* —5H **3**
Stuart Dri. *Hit* —6F **15**
Sturgeon Rd. *Hit* —3F **15**
Sturgeon's Way. *Hit* —3F **15**
Sturrock Way. *Hit* —1G **21**
Such Clo. *Let* —4H **11**
Summerfield Ct. *Stot* —3E **5**
Sunnyside. —2E 21
Sunnyside Rd. *Hit* —2E **21**
Sun St. *Bald* —3C **12**
Sun St. *Hit* —1C **20**
Sutcliffe Clo. *Stev* —1A **28**
Swale Clo. *Stev* —4A **24**
Swangley's La. *Kneb* —6E **31**
Swanstand. *Let* —1F **17**
Sweyns Mead. *Stev* —2C **28**
Swift Clo. *Let* —3E **11**
Swinburne Av. *Hit* —4A **14**
Swingate. *Stev* —4F **27**
Sycamore Clo. *St I* —3E **21**
Sycamores, The. *Bald* —3C **12**
Symonds Green. —2C 26
Symonds Grn. La. *Stev* —3C **26**
Symonds Grn. Rd. *Stev* —2C **26**
(in two parts)
Symonds Rd. *Hit* —5B **14**

Tabbs Clo. *Let* —4H **11**
Tabor Ct. *Let* —4D **10**
Tacitus Clo. *Stev* —1C **28**
Talbot St. *Hit* —5B **14**
Talbot Way. *Let* —2H **11**
Talisman St. *Hit* —6G **15**
Tall Trees. *St I* —3E **21**
Tamar Clo. *Stev* —4A **24**
Tarrant. *Stev* —6D **22**
Tates Way. *Stev* —5D **22**
Tatlers La. *Ast E* —4D **28**
Tatmorehills La. *Hit* —6A **20**
Taylor's Hill. *Hit* —1D **20**
Taylor's Rd. *Stot* —1F **5**
Taywood Clo. *Stev* —1F **31**
Tedder Av. *Henl* —4D **2**
Tees Clo. *Stev* —4H **23**

Telford Av. *Stev* —3B **28**
Templar Av. *Bald* —5D **12**
Temple Clo. *Hit* —3A **20**
Temple Ct. *Bald* —5D **12**
Temple End. —3A 20
Temple Gdns. *Let* —3A **12**
Tene, The. *Bald* —3D **12**
Tennyson Av. *Hit* —1G **21**
Thatchers End. *Hit* —5H **15**
Theobold Bus. Cen. *Hit*
—2E **15**
Third Av. *Let* —4A **12**
Thirlmere. *Stev* —5C **24**
Thistley La. *Gos* —5D **20**
Thornbury Clo. *Stev* —3E **31**
Three Star Cvn. Pk. *L Ston*
—6C **2**
Thristers Clo. *Let* —2D **16**
Thurlow Clo. *Stev* —5F **23**
Thurnall Clo. *Bald* —3D **12**
Tilehouse St. *Hit* —1C **20**
Tillers Link. *Stev* —1E **31**
Times Clo. *Hit* —3B **14**
Tintern Clo. *Stev* —4E **31**
Tippet Ct. *Stev* —6F **27**
Titmore Ct. *Hit* —5A **22**
Titmore Green. —5A 22
Titmus Clo. *Stev* —3G **27**
Todd's Green. —5C 22
Torquay Cres. *Stev* —2D **26**
Totts La. *Walk* —6H **25**
Tourist Information Cen.
(Stevenage) —5F **27**
Tower Clo. *L Wym* —4B **22**
Towers Rd. *Stev* —5F **27**
Towers, The. *Stev* —5F **27**
Town Gardens. —4G **27**
Townley. *Let* —1F **17**
Town Sq. *Stev* —4F **27**
Trafford Clo. *Stev* —6G **23**
Traherne Clo. *Hit* —2D **20**
Trajan Ga. *Stev* —6D **24**
Trent Clo. *Stev* —1G **27**
Trevor Rd. *Stev* —5E **15**
Triangle, The. *Hit* —1C **20**
Trigg Ter. *Stev* —3G **27**
Trinity Pl. *Stev* —3F **27**
Trinity Rd. *Stev* —3E **27**
Trinity Rd. *Stot* —2F **5**
Tristram Rd. *Hit* —3E **15**
Truemans Rd. *Hit* —3B **14**
Trumper Rd. *Stev* —6G **23**
Truro Ct. *Stev* —5H **23**
Trust Ind. Est. *Hit* —2E **15**
Tudor Clo. *Stev* —6E **23**
Tudor Ct. *Hit* —1B **20**
Turf La. *G'ley* —3D **22**
Turner Clo. *Stev* —5E **23**
Turnpike La. *Ickl* —2B **14**
Turpin's Ri. *Stev* —2D **30**
Turpin's Way. *Bald* —4D **12**
Twinwoods. *Stev* —5H **27**
Twitchell, The. *Bald* —3D **12**
(in two parts)
Twitchell, The. *Stev* —2F **27**
Tye End. *Stev* —3F **31**

Ullswater Clo. *Stev* —5C **24**
Underwood Rd. *Stev* —5E **23**
Unwin Clo. *Let* —1A **16**
Unwin Pl. *Stev* —6C **28**
Unwin Rd. *Stev* —6C **28**
Uplands. *Stev* —1D **28**
Uplands Av. *Hit* —1F **21**
Up. Maylins. *Let* —2E **17**
Upper Sean. *Stev* —6A **28**
Upper Stondon. —1A 8

Upperstone Clo. *Stot* —3F **5**
Up. Tilehouse St. *Hit* —6C **14**

Valerian Way. *Stev* —6D **24**
Vallansgate. *Stev* —2F **31**
Valley Rd. *Let* —4D **10**
Valley Way. *Stev* —1D **30**
Vardon Rd. *Stev* —1G **27**
Vaughan Rd. *Stot* —3E **5**
Verity Way. *Stev* —6A **24**
Verulam Rd. *Hit* —5D **14**
Vicarage Clo. *Arl* —1A **4**
Victoria Clo. *Stev* —2F **27**
Victoria Dri. *Stot* —4G **5**
Victoria Way. *Hit* —5B **14**
View Point. *Stev* —4C **26**
Vincent. *Let* —1E **17**
Vincent Ct. *Stev* —1D **26**
Vines, The. *Stot* —3E **5**
Vinters Av. *Stev* —4H **27**

Wadnall Way. *Kneb* —6G **31**
Walden End. *Stev* —5G **27**
Walkern. —6H 25
Walkern Rd. *B'tn* —6G **29**
Walkern Rd. *Stev* —2E **27**
(in two parts)
Walkers Ct. Bald —3D 12
(off High St.)
Wallace Way. *Hit* —3E **15**
Wallington Rd. *Bald* —3E **13**
Walnut Av. *Bald* —4E **13**
Walnut Clo. *Hit* —1E **21**
Walnut Clo. *Stot* —3F **5**
Walnut Tree Clo. *Stev* —5D **28**
Walnut Way. *Ickl* —1C **14**
Walpole Ct. *Stev* —4G **31**
Walsham Clo. *Stev* —4G **31**
Walsh Clo. *Hit* —6B **14**
Walsworth. —4F 15
Walsworth Rd. *Hit* —6D **14**
Waltham Rd. *Hit* —1D **20**
Wansbeck Clo. *Stev* —4A **24**
Warners Clo. *Stev* —6B **28**
Warren Clo. *Let* —4D **10**
Warren La. *Clot* —4F **13**
Warren Rd. *Clot* —6H **13**
Warren's Green. —1D 24
Warrensgreen La. *W'ton* —2C **24**
Warwick Rd. *Stev* —3C **28**
Watercress Clo. *Stev* —4D **28**
Waterdell La. *St I* —4D **20**
Water La. *Hit* —4D **14**
Waterloo La. *Hol* —5C **8**
Waterlow M. *L Wym* —4A **22**
Waters End. *Stot* —3E **5**
Watton Rd. *Kneb & Stev* —6E **31**
Waverley Clo. *Stev* —3E **31**
Waysbrook. *Let* —1D **16**
Waysmeet. *Let* —1D **16**
Weavers Way. *Bald* —3E **13**
Webb Clo. *Let* —6A **12**
Webb Ri. *Stev* —2H **27**
Wedgewood Rd. *Hit* —6F **15**
Wedgwood Ct. *Stev* —5C **24**
Wedgwood Ga. Ind. Est. *Stev*
—5B **24**
Wedgwood Pk. *Stev* —5C **24**
Wedgwood Way. *Stev* —6B **24**
Wedmore Rd. *Hit* —1E **21**
Wedon Way. *Byg* —5G **7**
Weedon Clo. *Henl* —4E **3**
Wellfield Clo. *Stev* —6B **24**
Wellingham Av. *Hit* —4B **14**
Wellington Rd. *Stev* —4C **28**
Wenham Ct. *Walk* —1H **29**